THE JURISDICTION OF THE PATRIARCHS OF THE MAJOR SEES IN ANTIQUITY AND IN THE MIDDLE AGES

A HISTORICAL COMMENTARY

THE CATHOLIC UNIVERSITY OF AMERICA
CANON LAW STUDIES
No. 276

The Jurisdiction of the Patriarchs of the Major Sees in Antiquity and in the Middle Ages

A Historical Commentary

BY THE
REVEREND THOMAS A. KANE, J.C.L.
PRIEST OF THE ARCHDIOCESE OF PHILADELPHIA

A DISSERTATION

SUBMITTED TO THE FACULTY OF THE SCHOOL OF CANON LAW OF THE CATHOLIC UNIVERSITY OF AMERICA IN PARTIAL FULFILLMENT OF THE REQUIREMENTS FOR THE DEGREE OF DOCTOR OF CANON LAW

THE CATHOLIC UNIVERSITY OF AMERICA PRESS
WASHINGTON, D. C.
1949

NIHIL OBSTAT:

Clemens V. Bastnagel, J.U.D., S.T.L.

Censor Deputatus

Washingtonii, D. C., die 16 decembris, 1948.

IMPRIMATUR:

✠ D. Card. Dougherty

Archiepiscopus Philadelphiensis

Philadelphiae, die 20 decembris, 1948.

Murray and Heister
Washington, D. C.

Printed by
Times and News Publishing Co.
Gettysburg, Pa., U.S.A.

Mariae
Reginae Cleri
hoc opus dedico

TABLE OF CONTENTS

TABLE OF CONTENTS (Continued)

TABLE OF CONTENTS (Continued)

FOREWORD

In antiquity, even before the I Council of Nicaea (325), there existed a custom by which certain metropolitan bishops exercised special powers over other metropolitans of a given region. That custom was subsequently confirmed by the Nicene Council in canon 6.

This preeminent jurisdictional rank of certain metropolitans may be designated by the term "patriarchal rank," inasmuch as they were eventually given the title "patriarch." In early times, however, this term "patriarch" was also used of other bishops besides those who actually enjoyed this superior jurisdiction over other metropolitans. A distinction must be made, therefore, between the jurisdictional superiority of the real patriarchs, and the honorary superiority of all the others who gloried in the use of this name.

Originally only three Bishops possessed this patriarchal jurisdiction. These were the Bishops of Rome, of Alexandria, and of Antioch. It was acquired at a later date by the Bishops of Constantinople and Jerusalem as well.

The scope of this dissertation will be to treat of the jurisdiction enjoyed by the Bishops of these five major sees as patriarchs, from the time that they acquired it up to the Council of Florence in the XV century. The work will be divided into two parts: the first, dealing with the early period up to the middle of the IX century; the second, with the subsequent period up to the Council of Florence.

The sources of the privileges of patriarchs have been expressly listed by Pope Nicholas I (858-867). He reduced them to three; namely, ancient custom, conciliar canons, and pontifical grant. The present writer has, therefore, endeavored to include the important canons, and the pontifical grants that he has been able to find. He has also cited ancient authors as witnesses of the customs observed in their day. If at times it was not possible to reach definite conclusions on some points, he has nevertheless set down his findings with the hope that at some future time new evidence may aid others in arriving at the correct answers. Should anything of importance have been omitted or misquoted, the writer hopes that the benevolent reader will supply for his failure.

The writer wishes to take this opportunity to express his sincere gratitude to His Eminence D. Cardinal Dougherty, Archbishop of Philadelphia, for the privilege of pursuing graduate studies in Canon Law at the Catholic University of America. He wishes to thank also the Rev. Dr. Clement V. Bastnagel and the Rev. Dr. Dionysius Holoweckyj who directed this dissertation for their kindness and help in seeing it through to completion, and he is especially grateful to all the members of the Faculty of the School of Canon Law for their assistance and interest during the course of his studies. Finally, to all his relatives and friends who have, whether by their prayers or in any other ways, aided him during his student days at Washington, the writer extends his sincere thanks.

PART ONE

The Patriarchs in Antiquity

CHAPTER I

The Patriarchal Rank in Antiquity

Article 1. The Testimony of the I Council of Nicaea (325)

The Bishops of Rome, of Alexandria, and of Antioch were referred to as true patriarchs by the I Council of Nicaea (325).[1] It is true, the Nicaean Fathers did not use the word "patriarch," a term which had not yet found its place in the terminology of the true Christian Church, but they did refer to a certain office, a certain position in the hierarchy, and the bishop who held such a position became known in later ages by the title of patriarch.[2]

A true patriarch held a position superior to that of metropolitans and all the other bishops of a given territory. He was the highest authority in that territory and, when there was question of a patriarch other than the Roman Pontiff, was subject only to the Pope, who holds the position of primate over the entire Church besides being Patriarch of the West. This was the patriarchal position that was recognized at Nicaea as belonging to the Bishops of Alexandria and Antioch, and also, according to most commentators, to the Bishop of Rome. These three Bishops were, therefore, the highest ranking ecclesiastics within the limits of their patriarchates.

---

[1] Canon 6: "De primatibus qui ad quasdam pertinent ciuitates. Antiqui mores obtineant qui apud Aegyptum sunt et Libiam et Penthapolim ut Alexandriae episcopus omnium habeat sollicitudinem, quia et urbis Romae episcopo similis mos est. Similiter autem et circa Antiochiam et in ceteris prouinciis priuilegia propria reseruentur metropolitanis aecclesiis. . . ."—Turner, *Ecclesiae Occidentalis Monumenta Juris Antiquissima*, fasciculus primus, pars altera (Oxonii: 1904), p. 120, secundum interpretationem Attici (hereinafter referred to as *Ecclesiae Occidentalis Monumenta*).

[2] ". . . sembra che si possa conchiudere, che per tutto il quarto secolo il nome di patriarca non fu data ad alcun vescovo in particolare per distintivo di si special dignità sopra gli altri vescovi."—Bianchi di Lucca, *Della Potestà e della Polizia della Chiesa* (2 vols., Torino, 1854-1857), II, 668 (hereafter cited as Bianchi).

The Bishops of Alexandria and Antioch were subject, in turn, only to the Bishop of Rome, who as the successor of St. Peter is the highest ranking ecclesiastic in the world.

Canon 6 of the I Council of Nicaea clearly stated that the Bishop of Alexandria had power over Egypt, Libya, and Pentapolis. Pope Innocent I (401-417) stated that the Council of Nicaea recognized this superior position as belonging to the Church of Antioch in its diocese.[3] And in the same canon of the Nicaean Council the patriarchal rank of Alexandria was compared to that of the Roman Bishop, ". . . quia et urbis Romae episcopo similis mos est. . . ." The Nicaean Fathers, therefore, recognized that the Roman See also enjoyed the patriarchal rank.

In stating that canon 6 instituted a comparison between the power there confirmed for the Bishop of Alexandria over his diocese and that enjoyed by the Roman Bishop over the regions of the West, one states the opinion of most of the commentators, but not the unanimous opinion.[4] A divergence in opinion arose from the words ". . . quia et urbis Romae episcopo similis mos est. . . ." In Greek, the sentence is rendered: ". . . επειδὴ και τῷ ἐν τῇ Ρωμῃ ἐπισκόπῳ τουτο σύνηθές ἐστιν. . . ."[5]

The word τουτο is the main word on which the controversy

[3] St. Innocentius I, *Ep. XXIV* (ad Alexandrum Antiochiae Episcopum): "Revolventes itaque auctoritatem Nicaenae synodi, quae una omnium per orbem terrarum explicat mentem sacerdotum, quae censuit de Antiochena ecclesia, cunctis fidelibus, ne dixerim sacerdotibus, esse necessarium custodire, qua super dioecesim suam praedictam ecclesiam, non super aliquam provinciam, recognoscimus constitutam. . . ."—Mansi, *Sacrorum Conciliorum Nova et Amplissima Collectio* (Editio Novissima, 53 vols. in 60, Florentiae, Venetiis, Parisiis, Arnhemii, Lipsiae: 1759-1927), tom. III, col. 1055 (hereinafter referred to as Mansi); Jaffé, *Regesta Pontificum Romanorum ab condita Ecclesia ad annum post Christum natum* MCXCVIII (2. ed. correctam et auctam auspiciis Gulielmi Wattenbach curaverunt S. Loewenfeld, F. Kaltenbrunner, P. Ewald, 2 Tomes in 1 Vol., Lipsiae, 1885-1888), n. 310 (hereinafter referred to as Jaffé); cf. Migne, *Patrologiae Cursus Completus, Series Latina* (221 vols., Parisiis: 1844-1864), XX, 547 (hereinafter referred to as *MPL*).

[4] Schroeder, *Disciplinary Decrees of the General Councils* (St. Louis: Herder & Co., 1937), p. 31 (hereafter cited as *General Councils*).

[5] Bruns, *Canones Apostolorum et Conciliorum Saeculorum IV, V, VI, VII* (Berolini: 1839), pars prior, p. 16.

hinges. Most of the commentators have applied this demonstrative pronoun to the power exercised by the Bishop of Rome over the regions of the West. They then interpret the canon to mean that the Bishop of Alexandria is to have over his diocese a power similar to that enjoyed by the Bishop of Rome over his diocese; and thus they institute a comparison between the Roman Bishop and the Alexandrian Bishop as Patriarchs. Among those who interpret canon 6 of Nicaea (325) in this manner are included Hefele- (1809-1893) Leclercq (1869-1945) and Cardinal Pitra (1812-1889).

Pitra in his commentary on canon 6 stated that it had been proven over and over that the rights and privileges of the three patriarchs were stated and confirmed by this law of Nicaea, with due acknowledgment always for the primacy of the Patriarch of Rome.[6]

Hefele-Leclercq noted that the Council of Nicaea recalled, for the support of its enactment, that the Bishop of Rome enjoyed rights analogous to those which it recognized and confirmed for the Bishop of Alexandria and Antioch; and they also indicated that the patriarchal rank was the only point on which an exclusive analogy between the three Bishops could be established.[7]

Others, however, apply the demonstrative τουτο to the supervision exercised by the Alexandrian Bishop over his patriarchate, interpreting the canon to mean that it was the custom of the Bishop of Rome to recognize that the Alexandrian Bishop enjoyed *this* superior rank over his diocese. Bouix (1808-1870) and Schroeder

---

[6] ". . . Hac vero lege nicaena declarari et confirmari trium patriarcharum iura et privilegia, salvo semper et incolumi romani patriarchae primatu, utpote totius ecclesiae norma, primitus et a Deo constituta, saepius iam comprobatum est. . . ."—Pitra, *Iuris Ecclesiastici Graecorum Historia et Monumenta* (2 toms., Romae: 1864-1868), I, 438.

[7] "A l'appui de son ordonnance, le concile de Nicée rappelle que l'évêque de Rome possède des droits analogues à ceux qu'il reconnaît a l'évêque d'Alexandrie (et à l'évêque d'Antioche). Il est évident que le concile ne fait pas ici allusion à la primauté universelle de l'évêque romain, mais simplement à son pouvoir patriarchal; c'est en effet le seul point de vue sous lequel on puisse établir une analogie entre Rome et Alexandrie ou Antioche; . . ."—Hefele-Leclercq, *Histoire des Conciles* (10 toms. in 19, Paris: Letouzey and Ané, 1907-1938), tom. I, page 560.

(1875-1942) may be cited as authors who defended this interpretation.

Bouix in a section devoted to the right interpretation of canon 6 of the Council of Nicaea wrote that the words which declared that the Roman Bishop had a similar custom were to be understood as pointing to a custom that the Roman Church had of recognizing the superior position over all Egypt for the Bishop of Alexandria.[8]

In his work on the disciplinary decrees of the General Councils, Schroeder commented that this controversy ought to be settled, not through any dependence upon translations, but from a consideration of "the grammatical structure of the Greek text." He added that a consideration of this text and also of the "logical sequence of the sentence" seems to demand that one interpret the passage as referring to "the custom of the Bishop of Rome to recognize the Alexandrian Bishop's right to have supervision of the Egyptian provinces."[9]

In addition to these three sees of Rome, Alexandria, and Antioch, the Council also referred to other Churches of superior rank when, in the same canon, it decreed: ". . . *similiter autem et circa Antiochiam et in ceteris prouinciis priuilegia propria reseruentur metropolitanis aecclesiis. . . .*" Thus it seems to have referred to the Bishop of Caesarea in Cappadocia in the civil diocese of Pontus, to the Bishop of Ephesus in the civil diocese of Asia, and to the Bishop of Heraclea in the civil diocese of Thrace. This is the general opinion, and it is supported, as Schroeder observed, by canon 2 of the I Council of Constantinople (381).[10]

---

[8] ". . . verba haec, *quandoquidem Romano Episcopo id consuetum est,* intelligi debent de consuetudine qua Romana Ecclesia solebat Alexandrinos Praesules agnoscere tanquam toti Aegypto praepositos. Proinde toto coelo errarunt, qui praedicta verba intellexerunt de consuetudine, qua Romana Sedes soleret Occidentis provincias regere. . . ."—Bouix, *Institutiones Juris Canonici in Varios Tractatus Divisae, Tractatus de Episcopo* (2. ed., 2 toms. bound in 1, Parisiis, Insulis, Tornaci: 1873), I, 414 (hereafter cited as Bouix, *De Episcopo*).

[9] *General Councils,* p. 31.

[10] *General Councils,* p. 32; Concilium Constantinopolitanum I (381), canon 2: "Episcopi ad ecclesias quae sunt ultra suam diocesim suosque limites ne accedant: sed secundum canones, Alexandriae quidem Episcopus Aegyptum

Although we are not told in detail by canon 6 of the Council of Nicaea (325) what the rights of these Bishops were, the common interpretation is that the Council wished to confirm for them the same superior jurisdiction over the dioceses of Thrace, Asia Prima, and Pontus that the Bishops of Alexandria and Antioch exercised over the dioceses of Egypt and the East.[11] However, their territory was less extensive than that of Rome, of Alexandria, or of Antioch, and it was closer to Constantinople.[12] With the rise to power of Constantinople, which was from its beginning a suffragan see of Heraclea, they were little by little reduced in importance. The title "exarch" became proper to them when the title "patriarch" was reserved for the bishops of the major sees.[13]

ARTICLE 2. THE ORIGIN OF THE PATRIARCHAL RANK

The I Council of Nicaea (325) did not institute the patriarchal rank. It found that rank already existing as an ancient institution,

---

solum regat. Orientis autem episcopi orientem solum administrent, servatis privilegiis ac praeeminentiis quae sunt in Nicaeni Concilii canonibus, Antiochenae ecclesiae. Et Asianae dioecesis episcopi quae sunt in sola Asiana administrata: et Thraciae episcopi Thraciam tantum regant et Pontanae Pontanam. . . ."—Mansi III, 559.

It is to be noted that this Council began as a particular council, but subsequently its definitions against Macedonius were raised to the status of those of an ecumenical council by the confirmation of Pope Damasus (366-384). The Pope, however, did not confirm the other purely disciplinary definitions. Pope Gregory the Great (590-604) referred to this in his letter to Eulogius, the Bishop of Alexandria, and Anastasius, the Bishop of Antioch, when he wrote: "Romana autem ecclesia eosdem canones vel gesta synodi illius hactenus non habet, nec accepit, in hoc autem eandem Synodum suscepit, quod est per eam contra Macedonium definitum."—*Registrum Epistolarum, Lib. VII, Ep. 31* (ad Eulogium Episcopum Alexandrinum et Anastasium episcopum Antiochenum): *Monumenta Germaniae Historica, Gregorii I Papae Registrum Epistolarum,* Tomus I, pars II (ed. L. Hartmann, Berolini: 1891), p. 479 (hereafter this collection will be cited as *MGH*); Jaffé, n. 1477; cf. *infra*, pp. 23-24 et 31.

[11] Schroeder, *General Councils,* p. 32.

[12] Thomassinus, *Vetus et Nova Ecclesiae Disciplina circa Beneficia et Beneficiarios* (3 parts in 10 vols., Magontiaci, 1787), Pars I, Lib. I, cap. 10, n. 8 (hereafter cited as Thomassinus).

[13] Kurtscheid, *Historia Iuris Canonici, Historia Institutorum,* Vol. I, *Ab Ecclesiae Fundatione usque ad Gratianum* (Romae: Officium Libri Catholici, 1941), p. 124 (hereafter cited as Kurtscheid); cf. *infra,* pp. 23 ff.

recognized it as such, and commanded, in canon 6, that there be no change, *"Antiqui mores obtineant. : . ."*

But, although the Council of Nicaea recognized the rank of these sees as a thing already existing, there is not to be found any text in any previous council that gave this special patriarchal power and jurisdiction over metropolitans to the Bishops of Alexandria and Antioch. Nor could the present writer find any testimony dating from the ante-Nicene period according to which any Bishop of Rome in virtue of his primacy *iure divino* over the entire Church made such an arrangement.[14]

As a result of this lack of more exact data regarding the origin of the patriarchal rank in the hierarchy, various explanations have been offered for it.

The oldest of these is one that comes from Pope Damasus (366-384). He attributed the superior position of the patriarchal Churches of Alexandria and Antioch to their relationship to St. Peter.[15]

---

[14] "Non trovandosi pertanto in pria del concilio di Nicea alcun altro concilio in cui ai vescovi alessandrino ed antiocheno prescritta fosse questa potesta di giurisdizione sopra i metropolitani delle diocesi di Egitto e di Oriente, . . ."—Bianchi, II, 149; "Antiquissimum et primum exemplum, quo metropolita speciali Romani Pontificis concessione ad gradum superiorem evectus est, vicariatus Thessalonicensis praebet, quatenus metropolitae hujus civitatis vi delegationis Romanorum Pontificum iura primatialia in provincias Illyriae exercebant."—Kurtscheid, I, 127.

[15] "Est ergo prima Petri Apostoli sedes Romana Ecclesia; non habens maculam, neque rugam, nec aliquid hujusmodi. Secunda autem sedes apud Alexandriam beati Petri nomine a Marco ejus discipulo, atque evangelista consecrata est. Ipseque in Aegypto directus a Petro Apostolo, verbum veritatis praedicavit, et gloriosum consummavit martyrium. Tertia vero sedes apud Antiochiam item beatissimi Apostoli Petri habetur honorabilis, eo quod illic, priusquam Romam venisset, habitavit: Et illic primum nomen Christianorum novellae gentis exortum est."—Mansi, VIII, 160.

It is to be noted that this text, which now is rightfully attributed to Pope Damasus, was formerly associated with the so called Gelasian Decretals. It appears thus in Mansi. For fuller information on the attribution of this to Pope Damasus see Grisar, *History of Rome and the Popes in the Middle Ages* (Authorized English translation edited by Luigi Cappadelta, 3 vols., London, 1911-1912), I, p. 335, footnote 2 (hereinafter this work will be referred to as *History of Rome*).

In commenting on this teaching of Pope Damasus, Grisar (1845-1932) stated:

> Various views have been offered regarding the origin of the patriarchal dignity. The above Papal decree has the great advantage of being the earliest, and of emanating from the best authority. Evidently the idea prevailed at Rome and in the West, and with good reason, that the superiority of the Patriarchs had its foundation in a closer share of the power and dignity of the centre and source of church unity at Rome, and was not the outcome of the successful efforts at self-aggrandizement of the Patriarchs themselves or of the political rank of their sees. Hereby, of course, the view was not excluded that the historical commencement of the pre-eminence of Alexandria and Antioch was also largely a result of the good work done by these churches for the spread of the faith throughout their wide spheres of influence. As a fact, both became parent-churches to numerous bishoprics of their own foundation. Unfortunately, precise data are wanting which might enable us to trace the earliest historical development of their patriarchal institutions.[16]

Pope Innocent I (401-417) in a letter to Alexander, the Bishop of Antioch, after speaking of the position of higher authority enjoyed by the Church of Antioch over its diocese, referred to the reason why the Antiochene Church had this superior rank. He gave as the reason the fact that Antioch was the first See of the first Apostle.[17]

Pope Nicholas I (858-867), in his letter of reply to the Bulgarians, wrote that they must be truly considered Patriarchs who obtain through the succession of Pontiffs the Apostolic Sees, that is, they who preside over the Churches which the Apostles instituted, namely Rome, Alexandria, and Antioch. He then treated of the relationship of St. Peter to these sees.[18]

---

[16] *History of Rome,* I, 340.

[17] Innocentius I, *Ep. XXIV* (ad Alexandrum Episcopum Antiochenum): . . . "Unde advertimus, non tam pro civitatis magnificentia hoc eidem attributum, quam quod prima primi apostoli sedes esse monstretur, . . ."—*MPL,* XX, 548; Mansi, III, 1055; Jaffé, n. 310.

[18] *Ep. XCIX,* cap. 92: "Desideratis nosse, quot sint veraciter patriarchae. Veraciter illi habendi sunt patriarchae, qui sedes apostolicas per successiones

It must not be denied, however, that the division of the Roman provinces could have served as an occasion or as a natural help, which the early Church in forming the ecclesiastical hierarchy made use of in a secondary way.[19] For in Apostolic times the three principal cities of the Roman Empire were Rome, Alexandria, and Antioch. Rome was the head of the entire Empire; Alexandria, the metropolis of Egypt; and Antioch, the metropolis of Asia and the East. Kurtscheid (1877-1941) stated that there was a relationship between the patriarchal dignity and the division of the Roman Empire. He noted that patriarchs or exarchs existed in those metropolises which were the capitals of the civil dioceses, namely in Antioch, the capital of the civil diocese of the East; in Alexandria, the capital of Egypt; in Ephesus, the capital of Asia; in Caesarea in Cappadocia, the capital of Pontus; and in Heraclea, the capital of Thrace.[20]

---

pontificum optinent, id est qui illis praesunt ecclesiis, quas apostoli instituisse probantur, Romanam videlicet, Alexandrinam et Antiochenam. Romanam, quam sanctorum principes apostolorum Petrus ac Paulus et praedicatione sua instituerunt et pro Christi amore fuso proprio sanguine sacraverunt; Alexandrinam, quam evangelista Marcus discipulus et de baptismate Petri filius a Petro missus instituit et domino Christo cruore dicavit; Antiochenam, in qua conventu magno sanctorum facto primum fideles dicti sunt Christiani et quam beatus Petrus, priusquam Romam veniret, per annos aliquot gubernavit. . . ."—*MGH,* Epistolarum Tom. VI, *Epistolae Karolini Aevi,* Tom. IV (ed. E. Perels, Berolini: Apud Weidmannos, 1925), p. 596; Jaffé, n. 2812.

[19] Wernz-Vidal, *Ius Canonicum* (7 toms. bound in 9, Romae: 1928-1943), Tom. II (3. ed., 1943), p. 641 (hereinafter referred to as Wernz-Vidal).

A distinction must be made between a cause and an occasion. A cause is defined as "principium, quod suo influxo positivo determinat existentiam alterius rei"; whereas "occasio nec influit in effectum nec requiritur, ut effectus existat, sed est id, ad cujus praesentiam aliquid fit."—Hickey, *Summula Philosophiae Scholasticae* (3 vols., Dublini: Apud Brown et Nolan, Vol. I, ed. altera, 1908; Vol. II, 1904; Vol. III, pars prior, 1905), I, 429, 431.

[20] "Concilium Nicaenum, . . . in canone 6 loquitur de ecclesiis Alexandrina, Antiochena, Romana, quibus superiorem jurisdictionem in plures provincias ecclesiasticas agnoscit; similiter in aliis eparchiis ecclesiis principatum . . . servari vult; praedictus canon 6 igitur secundum rem illum gradum hierarchicum significat, cui postea titulus, 'patriarchae' attribuitur.

"Haec quoque dignitas relationem habet ad divisionem imperii Romani,

Sägmuller (1860-1942), in his treatment of the parallelism between the ecclesiastical and political territory, remarked that the Apostles and their successors preached the Gospel at first in the large cities of the Roman Empire, namely, in Antioch, Ephesus, Athens, Corinth, Rome, and other cities; and that from these capitals and metropolitan centers Christianity spread into the civil provinces. He added that it was natural for these more important cities and political districts of the Empire to become also of greater importance in the ecclesiastical division of territory. And so he concluded that from such an interplay of ecclesiastical and political elements there arose the territories subject to the patriarchs and exarchs, the provinces of the metropolitans and the dioceses of the bishops.[21]

The origin of the patriarchal rank, then, seems to be traceable to many elements. Among these one should point out the special relationship of Rome, Alexandria, and Antioch to St. Peter, as many papal letters declare; it should also be mentioned that the territorial arrangement within the Roman Empire could have served as an occasion for the rise of the Patriarchates.

It is to be noted, however, that the "Church did not slavishly adapt the civil order to the grades of the hierarchy. Indeed, it

---

etsi haec ratio non fuerit motivum unicum. Nam patriarchas resp. exarchas in illis metropolibus invenimus, quae erant capita dioecesium civilium scilicet: d. Orientis (Antiochia), d. Aegypti (Alexandria), d. Asiae (Ephesus), d. Ponti (Caesarea in Cappadocia), d. Thraciae (Heraclea)."—Kurtscheid, I, 120.

[21] "Die Apostel haben das Evangelium zunächst in den grossen Städten des römischen Reiches, in Antiochien, Ephesus, Athen, Korinth, Rom u.a., verkündet. So hielten es auch ihre Nachfolger. Von solchen Hauptstädten und Metropolen (μητροπόλεις) aus verbreitete sich dann das Christentum in den politischen Provinzen (επαρχίαι). Naturgemäss wurden da die hervorragenderen und hervorragendsten Städte und die grösseren und grössten politischen Bezirke (διοικήσεις) des römischen Reiches auch für die kirchliche Einteilung von grosser Bedeutung. Aus solchem Zusammenspiel kirchlicher und politischer Gründe entstanden die Sprengel der Patriarchen und Exarchen, die Provinzen der Metropoliten und die Diözesen der Bischöfe. Doch waren diese kirchenpolitischen Auswirkungen nicht zwingend."—Sägmuller, *Lehrbuch des katholischen Kirchenrechts* (4. ed., 1 Vol. in 4 parts [incomplete], Freiburg im Breisgau: Herder & Co., 1925-1934) Erster Band, vierter Teil (1934), pp. 589-590 (hereafter cited as *Lehrbuch*).

bravely resisted and vindicated its independence when false theories and perverse practices were introduced from the division of the civil provinces."[22] Pope Innocent I (401-417) in his letter to Alexander, the Bishop of Antioch, stated that the divisions of the civil provinces decided upon by the Emperor, so that two metropoles might be made, were not to be followed by the nomination of two metropolitan bishops. Rather were the metropolitan bishops to be nominated as heretofore, *secundum pristinum provinciarum morem.*[23]

Canon 17 of the Council of Chalcédon (451) stated that if any city had been raised in rank or afterwards should be raised in rank on imperial authority, the order of ecclesiastical parishes should follow the civil and public forms.[24] But in another canon, which repeated the regulation stated by Pope Innocent I referred to above, removal from office was threatened to anyone who, acting on the authority of imperial letters but contrary to the regulations of the Church, should divide one province into two, so that from this division two metropolitans would exist in one province.[25]

ARTICLE 3. THE EXTENT OF THE PATRIARCHAL TERRITORY

The extent of the territory over which the Pope had jurisdiction as Supreme Pontiff comprised all of Christendom. As Patriarch, however, he exercised a more immediate control over a certain

[22] Wernz-Vidal, II, 641.

[23] *Ep. XXIV* (ad Alexandrum Episcopum Antiochenum): ". . . quod sciscitaris, utrum divisis imperiali judicio provinciis, ut duo metropoles fiant, sic duo metropolitani episcopi debeant nominari: non vere visum est, ad mobilitatem necessitatum mundanarum Dei ecclesiam commutari, honoresque aut divisiones perpeti, quas pro suis causis faciendas duxerit imperator. Ergo secundum pristinum provinciarum morem, metropolitanos episcopos convenit nominari."—Jaffé, n. 310; *MPL*, XX, 547; Mansi, III, 1055.

[24] Canon 17: ". . . Sin autem etiam civitas aliqua ab imperatoria auctoritate innovata est, vel deinceps innovata fuerit, civiles et publicas formas ecclesiasticarum quoque parochiarum ordo consequatur."—Mansi, VII, 366.

[25] Canon 12: "Pervenit ad nos, quod quidam, cum praeter ritus ecclesiasticos ad potentatus accessissent, per pragmaticas unam provinciam in duas diviserunt: ut ex eo duo essent metropolitani in eadem provincia. Statuit ergo sacra synodus, ne episcopus deinceps tale quid audeat: quoniam is qui hoc aggreditur, a suo gradu excidit. . . ."—Mansi, VII, 363.

portion of the Christian world. This Patriarchal authority was also exercised by the Bishops of Alexandria and Antioch over their respective territories, while they remained subject, of course, to the Roman Bishop as supreme Pontiff. The territory over which these Bishops exercised patriarchal jurisdiction came to be referred to as their diocese.[26]

In this article the ancient extent of the territory of the patriarchate of Rome will be described. The extent of the patriarchal territory of Alexandria will be described as it was in 325. The extent of the ancient patriarchate of Antioch will also be indicated.

Section 1. The Patriarchal Territory of Rome

The I Council of Nicaea in canon 6 stated nothing in detail of the extent of the territory over which the Roman Bishop ruled as Patriarch. But Rufinus (330-410), a priest of Aquileia, in his *Historia Ecclesiastica* gave the canon in the following form:

> Et ut apud Alexandriam, et in urbe Roma, vetusta consuetudo servetur, ut vel ille Aegypti, vel hic suburbicariarum Ecclesiarum sollicitudinem gerat.[27]

This testimony of Rufinus gave rise to a controversy as to the extent of the territory over which the Roman Bishop had that particular jurisdiction of which the canon treated. The controversy centered around the meaning of the words "suburbicariarum ecclesiarum."

Before recounting the opinions of the authors as to the proper interpretation of these words, one should point briefly to the

---

[26] "Territorium patriarcharum a concilio Constantinopolitano I (381) vocatur 'dioecesis,' quo termino etiam exarcharum territorium correspondens dioecesi civili significabatur. Idem clare ostendit lex Justiniani anno 530 (L. 29 C. I 4) modum appellandi praescribens, quae praeter metropolitae tantum patriarchae territorium 'dioecesim' nominat."—Kurtscheid, I, 122; cf. Funk, *A Manual of Church History* (2 vols., edited by W. H. Kent, London: Burns, Oates & Washbourne, Ltd., 1938), I, 56-58 (hereinafter referred to as *Church History*).

[27] Rufinus, *Historia Ecclesiastica,* liber I, caput 6—*MPL,* XXI, 473.

political setup in Italy during the fourth century. According to Grisar, "the political diocese of Italy was divided during the fourth century into two halves: one, called *dioecesis suburbicaria,* with Sicily, Sardinia, and Corsica; the other, *dioecesis annonaria,* or *dioecesis Italiae,* i.e., of the peninsula as far as the neighborhood of Pisa and Ravenna. Two vicars directed these divisions. One, for the south, lived in Rome, and was called *Vicarius in urbe,* or *urbis;* the other in Milan, and was called *Vicarius Italiae.* Rome had also its *Praefectus urbi* for the city itself and its environs as far as the hundredth milestone."[28]

Concerning the words *suburbicariarum ecclesiarum* of Rufinus, there were those who interpreted these words as referring to that territory which lay within 100 miles of Rome, and over which the *Praefectus urbi* had authority; and there were others who held that the canon referred to the territory over which the *Vicarius urbis* was placed, a territory which comprised ten provinces of Italy.[29]

However, a very ancient codex indicated that the extent of the territory reached farther than either of these opinions allowed, for it related canon 6 of the I Council of Nicaea (325) in a form which contained the added words, *et omnem provinciam.*[30]

Balsamon and Zonaras, twelfth century commentators on this canon, recognized the patriarchal power of the Bishop of Rome as extending to all the West. Thus Balsamon (1140-1195) wrote that canon 6 of Nicaea stated that the Bishop of Rome presided over

[28] *History of Rome,* I, p. 344, footnote 2.

[29] "Quae verba Rufini Jacob Gothofredus (d. 1652) et Salmasius (d. 1653) intellexerunt de territorio Romae intra 100 milliarium, cui praefectus urbi praeerat; alii ut Sirmond (d. 1651), de territorio vicarii urbis, quod 10 provincias Italiae complectebatur."—Kurtscheid, I, 123.

[30] "Codex Antiquissimus V. C. Henrici Justelli p. 284 bibliothecae canonicae hunc titulum exhibet: 'De primatu ecclesiae Romanae et aliarum civitatum episcopis.' Dein sequitur canon: 'Antiqui moris est ut urbis Romae episcopus habeat principatum, ut suburbicaria loca et omnem provinciam sua sollicitudine gubernet. Quae vero apud Aegyptum sunt, Alexandriae episcopus omnem habeat sollicitudinem. Similiter autem et circa Antiochiam et in caeteris provinciis privilegia propria serventur metropolitanis ecclesiis. . . .' "—Mansi, II, 688, Observatio P. Labbé.

the western provinces.[31] And Zonaras stated that the Bishop of Rome obtained by custom the rule over the western provinces.[32] St. Augustine (354-430) and St. Basil (330-379) called the Bishop of Rome the primate of the Western Church.[33]

In the *Novellae* the Emperor Justinian I (527-565) gave expression to the same idea. For, in referring to the ecclesiastical division of the whole world, he named only the Roman Pontiff in addition to the four eastern Patriarchs, thus indicating that the jurisdiction of the Roman Pontiff as Patriarch extended to all the West.[34]

Pope Benedict XIV (1740-1758) in his *De Synodo Dioecesana* referred to other authors who were of the opinion that the phrase *suburbicariae ecclesiae,* as used by Rufinus, embraced all the regions of the West.[35]

---

[31] *Balsamonis et Zonarae, in canones SS. Apostolorum, Conciliorum et in Epistolas Canonicas SS. Patrum commentaria:* "Praesens . . . canon inquit . . . Romanus episcopus praeest occidentalibus provinciis."—Migne, *Patrologiae Cursus Completus, Series Graeca* (161 vols., Parisiis: 1856-1866), Vol. CXXXVII, col. 243 (hereafter cited as *MPG*) ; Kurtscheid, I, 123.

[32] *Op. cit.;* "Ecclesiae Romanae praeses in occidentales provincias principatum consuetudine obtinet. . . ."—*MPG,* CXXXVII, 254; Kurtscheid, I, 123.

[33] Kurtscheid, I, 123.

[34] Imp. Iustinianus Aug. Iohanni pp. per Orientem. "Haereticos vero et illi dixerunt et nos dicimus eos qui diversarum sunt haeresium; quibus coniungimus et connumeramus et qui Nestorii Iudaicam sequuntur vesaniam et Eutychianistas et Acephalos, qui Dioscori et Severi mala secta languent Manichaei et Apolinaris renovantium inpietatem, et ad haec omnes qui non sunt membrum sanctae dei catholicae et apostolicae ecclesiae, in qua omnes concorditer sanctissimi (episcopi et) totius orbis terrarum patriarchae, et Hesperiae Romae et huius regiae civitatis et Alexandriae et Theopoleos et Hierosolymorum, et omnes qui sub eis constituti sunt sanctissimi episcopi apostolicam praedicant fidem atque traditionem."—*Corpus Iuris Civilis,* Vol. III, *Novellae* (5. ed., recognovit Rudolfus Schoell, absolvit Gulielmus Kroll, Berolini: Apud Weidmannos, 1928), pp. 517-518. Cf. N. (109. pr.).

[35] "Emmanuel a Schelstrate, . . . Pagius ad annum 325. num. 34, Carolus A Paulo in sua *Geographia sacra,* aliique passim, considerantes VI canonem Nicaenum, seu verius explicationem, quam ei adjecit Rufinus, . . . non immerito existimant, nomine suburbicariarum ecclesiarum, quarum specialem sollicitudinem habet Romanus Pontifex, non solum intelligi provinciam Romanam, sed omnes comprehendi Occidentis regiones, quae Romano Pontifici, tamquam Patriarchae, parebant; siquidem Concilium Nicaenum, et Rufinum, non de Metropolitico, sed de Patriarchico jure loqui, ex contextu liquet, atque exinde conficitur, suburbicarias regiones, de quibus Rufinus,

The regions of the West which after the division of the Empire in the fourth century constituted the patriarchal territory of the Bishop of Rome are listed as follows by Grisar: the Patriarchate "embraced the Prefecture of Italy, those of the two Gauls, and that of Eastern Illyricum. The first Prefecture contained the three political 'dioceses' of Italy, Western Illyricum, and Africa; the second Prefecture included the 'dioceses' of Spain, of the *Septem Provinciae* (i.e., Gaul, Belgium, *Germania prima* and *secunda,* etc.), and Britain. The third Prefecture was that of *Illyricum Orientale,* with the 'diocese' of Macedonia and Dacia, which since Theodosius I (379-395) had formed a portion of the Eastern Empire."[36]

Section 2. The Patriarchal Territory of Alexandria

The territory mentioned in canon 6 of the I Council of Nicaea as subject to the Bishop of Alexandria embraced Egypt (considered in the narrower sense), Libya, and Pentapolis. In referring to Egypt, the Council included also Upper Egypt or Thebais, for this, according to Hefele (1809-1893), was certainly under the jurisdiction of the Bishop of Alexandria in 325.[37] This Bishop, therefore, at that time had jurisdiction over the civil diocese of Egypt which was made up of the four civil provinces of Egypt (in its narrower meaning), of Libya, of Pentapolis, and of Thebais. Later on the civil diocese was divided into six provinces; namely,

---

non solum intra centesimum ab urbe lapidem non esse conclusas, sed ad universum porrigi Occidentem."—Benedictus XIV, *De Synodo Dioecesana* (secunda Parmensis ed., 2 toms., Parmae: 1764), lib. 2, cap. 2, n. 2 (hereinafter referred to as *De Synodo Dioecesana*).

[36] *History of Rome,* I, 344; "Illyricum, una ex praefecturis imperii Romani cum capitali Sirmium, anno 379 divisa est in Illyricum Orientale, cui praefectus praetorio Thessalonicae residens praeerat, quam partem Gratianus cessit Theodosio imperatori Orientis, et in Illyricum Occidentale, quod sub vicario Sirmii residente manebat pars imperii Occidentis resp. praefecturae Italiae. Dum totius Illyriae provinciae potestati patriarchali Romani Pontificis erant subiectae, post divisionem patriarchae Constantinopolitani in partem orientalem iurisdictionem suam extendere coeperunt. Quare Summi Pontifices, ut melius iura ecclesiae Romanae servarent, metropolitam Thessalonicensem vicarium suum constituerunt."—Kurtscheid, I, 126.

[37] *Histoire des Conciles,* I, 555.

Pentapolis (*Lybia superior*), *Lybia inferior,* Thebais, Egypt, Augustamnica (the eastern part of Egypt), and Arcadia or Eptanomis (the middle part of Egypt).[38]

A question may be asked concerning the ecclesiastical division of the civil diocese in 325. Was it, for ecclesiastical purposes, also divided into several ecclesiastical provinces, each with its own metropolitan, who was in turn subject to the superior metropolitan at Alexandria; or was this civil diocese regarded by the Church as forming only one ecclesiastical province, over which the Alexandrian Bishop was the only metropolitan? Hefele stated it as incontestable that the civil provinces of Egypt (in its narrower signification), of Libya, of Pentapolis, and of Thebais, all subject to the Bishop of Alexandria, were also ecclesiastical provinces each having its own metropolitan.[39] Among other proofs listed in support of this view, Hefele included a reference to the general rule confirmed by the Council of Nicaea in canon 4, which rule determined that an ecclesiastical province under a metropolitan should correspond to each civil province. He stated that there is nothing to prove that Libya, Pentapolis, and Thebais were exceptions to this general rule.[40]

Section 3. The Patriarchal Territory of Antioch

If one considers canon 2 of the I Council of Constantinople (381), one can see that the Bishop of Antioch, at least at that time, ruled over that territory whose limits corresponded with those of the civil diocese of the East.[41] This civil diocese of the East was divided into provinces. According to Hefele, who took his information from Böcking, *Notitia dignitatum,* these provinces were Palestine, Phoenicia, Syria, Cilicia, Cyprus, Arabia, Isauria, Palaestina salutaris, Palaestina II, Phoenicia Lybani, Eufratensis,

---

[38] *Loc. cit.*

[39] "Il est donc incontestable que les provinces civiles de l'Egypte, de la Libye, de la Pentapole et de la Thebaide, toutes soumises a l'eveque d'Alexandrie, etaient pourvues de provinces ecclesiastiques avec leurs metropolitains propres."—*Histoire des Conciles,* I, 558.

[40] *Ibid.,* p. 557.

[41] *Supra,* pp. 6-7; *Histoire des Conciles,* I, 559.

Syria salutaris, Osrhoëna, and Cilicia II.[42] But Hefele also indicated that there was some uncertainty in his mind as to the number of civil provinces into which, *at the time of the I Council of Nicaea (325),* the civil diocese of the East was divided.[43]

There was no uncertainty, however, about the fact that canon 6 of the Council of Nicaea (325) "recognized in the Bishop of Antioch, a supremacy extending over several provinces, each one provided with a metropolitan."[44] Thus Palestine was an ecclesiastical province, whose metropolitan see was Caesarea. Caesarea, however, remained subject to the superior jurisdiction of the Bishop of Antioch. St. Jerome (ca. 343-420) bore witness to this arrangement.[45] And Pope Innocent I (401-417) in a letter to Alexander, the Bishop of Antioch, by stating that Antioch had authority, not over a single province, but over the entire diocese, testified to the fact that there were many ecclesiastical provinces in the ecclesiastical diocese of the East.[46]

Schroeder, in his commentary on the I Council of Nicaea (325), canon 6, stated that ". . . from remote antiquity the Bishop of Antioch had exercised a certain jurisdiction over many provinces in the eastern extremity of the Roman Empire. Tradition has it that his supremacy extended even beyond the limits of the Empire. At any rate, the Council of Constantinople (381) in canon 2 restricted his jurisdiction to the civil diocese of the Orient, which at that time embraced fifteen civil provinces. Whether or not this civil diocese comprised all of these provinces in 325 is a matter of little importance here. Certain it is that our canon attributes to the Bishop of Antioch a supremacy or jurisdiction over many provinces, each having its own metropolitan. It would seem, then, that the Council recognized and secured to him the same juris-

---

[42] *Histoire des Conciles,* I, 559.

[43] "Quel que soit le nombre des provinces civiles que comprenait le diocese d'Orient en 325. . . ."—*loc. cit.*

[44] *Loc. cit.*

[45] *Liber contra Joannem Hierosolymitanum ad Pammachium:* "Ni fallor, hoc ibi (i.e., apud Nicaenum Concilium) decernitur, ut Palaestinae metropolis Caesaria sit et totius Orientis Antiochia."—*MPL,* XXIII, 389.

[46] *Ep. XXIV* (ad Alexandrum Antiochiae Episcopum)—Jaffé, n. 310; *MPL,* XX, 547; cf. *infra,* p. 40.

diction that it recognized and secured to the Bishop of Alexandria over the provinces of Egypt."[47]

ARTICLE 4. THE PATRIARCHATE OF JERUSALEM

The I Council of Nicaea (325) took cognizance of a custom and ancient tradition whereby the Bishop of Jerusalem was held in honor, and ordered that he be given the pre-eminence of honor over the other bishops of his province, but without prejudice to the dignity and the rights of the metropolitan, the Bishop of Caesarea.[48]

At the time of the Council of Nicaea, Palestine was a single province for the purpose both of the ecclesiastical and of the civil administration. Its status, however, was changed for the civil administration by Theodosius the Great (379-395), who divided it into two provinces; and again by Arcadius (395-408), the son of Theodosius, who divided it into three provinces.[49]

The ecclesiastical arrangement in Palestine after 325 and during the time that it existed as a single province provided that Jerusalem have the status of a suffragan see of Caesarea, and that Caesarea be subject to the Bishop of Antioch, who had that over-metropolitan jurisdiction which subsequently came to be called the patriarchal rank.[50] This ecclesiastical arrangement was not changed when Theodosius divided the province of Palestine into two, and Arcadius into three provinces, for the purposes of the civil administration; it remained as it had been.

---

[47] *General Councils*, p. 32; cf. *supra*, p. 7, concerning the attitude of Pope Damasus and Pope Gregory the Great towards those canons of the I Council of Constantinople (381) which did not pertain to the definition of the faith against Macedonius.

[48] Canon 7: "De episcopo Heliae id est Hierusolimitano. Quoniam consuetudo preualuit et antiqua traditio ut honoraretur episcopus Heliae, habeat honorem, metropolitane ciuitatis dignitate seruata."—Turner, *Ecclesiae Occidentalis Monumenta,* fasciculus primus, pars altera, p. 122, secundum interpretationem Caeciliani.

[49] Bianchi, II, 675 and 677.

[50] Concilium Nicaenum I, canon 7—Turner, *Ecclesiae Occidentalis Monumenta,* fasciculus primus, pars altera, p. 122; St. Innocentius I, *Ep. XXIV* (ad Alexandrum Antiochiae Episcopum)—Jaffé, n. 310; *MPL,* XX, 547; Mansi, III, 1054-1055; St. Hieronymus, *Liber contra Joannem Hierosolymitanum ad Pammachium—MPL,* XXIII, 389.

At the time of the Council of Ephesus (431), Palestine was still a single province as far as the ecclesiastical administration was concerned. Pope Leo the Great (440-461) in a letter to Maximus, the Bishop of Antioch (449-455), referred to it as such.[51]

In the year 421 Juvenal became the Bishop of Jerusalem, and during his incumbency Jerusalem at least *de facto* acquired the rank of a patriarchal see. At the time of the Council of Ephesus (431) he tried to take advantage of favorable circumstances to withdraw Palestine from the jurisdiction of Antioch and to acquire for himself the position of supremacy over it. St. Cyril, Bishop of Alexandria (412-444), opposed him, however, and reported the affair to Rome. As a consequence the attempt of Juvenal failed, at least for that time.[52] But although this attempt of Juvenal ended in failure, he did not give up. At the Robber Synod of Ephesus (449) he made friends with Chrysaphius, a eunuch who was powerful with Theodosius II (408-450), and with the help of this man he obtained by imperial rescript not only the absolute administration of Palestine, but also that of Arabia and Phoenicia, which accordingly were separated from the Patriarchate of Antioch.[53]

---

[51] St. Leo I, *Ep. CXIX* (ad Maximum Antiochenum Episcopum): ". . . de Ephesina Synodo . . . Juuenalis episcopus ad optinendum Palaestinae Prouinciae principatum credidit se posse proficere. . . ."—Schwartz, *Acta Conciliorum Oecumenicorum,* Tomus II, *Concilium Universale Chalcedonense,* Vol. IV (Berolini et Lipsiae: Walter de Gruyter & Co., 1932), p. 74, secundum collectionem Grimanicam (hereinafter Tomus II of this work will be referred to as *Concilium Universale Chalcedonense*); Jaffé, n. 495.

[52] St. Leo I, *Ep. CXIX:* "Subripiendi enim occasiones non praetermittit ambitio, et quotiens ob occurrentes causas generalis congregatio facta fuerit sacerdotum, difficile est ut cupiditas improborum non aliquid supra mensuram suam moliatur appetere, sicut etiam de Ephesina Synodo, . . . Juvenalis episcopus ad optinendum Palaestinae prouinciae principatum credidit se posse proficere et insolentes ausus per commenticia scripta firmare. Quod sanctae memoriae Cyrillus Alexandrinus episcopus merito perhorrescens, scriptis suis mihi quid praedicti cupiditas ausa sit, indicauit et sollicita prece multum poposcit ut nulla illicitis conatibus praeberetur assensio."—Schwartz, *Concilium Universale Chalcedonense,* Vol. IV, p. 74, secundum collectionem Grimanicam; Jaffé, n. 495.

[53] ". . . nel proditorio e latrocinal conciliabolo efesino tenuto l'anno 449; . . . si fece merito appresso Crisafio eunuco potentissimo coll' imperador Teodosio, . . . Col mezzo adunque di costui ottenne Giovenale per rescritto

At the Council of Chalcedon (451) Juvenal finally succeeded in obtaining from the Council the recognition of his see as a patriarchal see. After having forced Maximus to come to an agreement with him on the matter, both parties proposed the agreement to the Council. In *Actio VII* of the Council this agreement was accepted by the bishops, and even by the papal legates *pro bono pacis.*

According to the terms of this agreement Palestine was separated from the jurisdiction of Antioch and divided into three provinces. Jerusalem took the place of Caesarea as the first see, but with this difference: Caesarea had been the metropolitan see at the head of a single province, but Jerusalem became the head of three provinces. Thus Jerusalem acquired an over-metropolitan or a patriarchal jurisdiction.

The pertinent references to this in *Actio VII* of the Council may be divided as follows: first, the proposing of the agreement;[54] second, the consent of the papal legates *pro bono pacis;*[55] third,

---

dell' imperadore non solo il reggimento assoluto della Palestina, ma anche dell' Arabia e della Fenicia, provincie smembrate dal patriarcato antiocheno." —Bianchi, II, 680.

[54] "Maximus reuerentissimus episcopus Antiochiae Syriae dixit: Placuit mihi et reuerentissimo episcopo Juuenali quos post multam altercationem ad concordiam ut sedem Antiochinae urbis, quae est sancti Petri, habere duo Fenices et Arabiam, sedem uero Hierosolymitanam habere tres Palaestinas, si tamen id uenerabili patri nostro archiepiscopo Romae majoris Leoni placuerit, qui cupit ubique sanctorum patrum canones infringibles permanere. Et rogamus ex sententia uestrae magnificentiae et sanctae synodi per scripturam haec roborari.

"Juuenalis uenerabilis episcopus Hierosolymitanus dicit: Eadem mihi placuit ut sanctam quidem Christi Anastasim tres Palaestinas habere, sedem uero Antiochiae duas Fenices et Arabiam. Rogo et ego ex sententia uestrae magnificentiae et sanctae synodi haec roborari."—Schwartz, *Concilium Universale Chalcedonense,* Vol. II, pars altera (Berolini et Lipsiae: Walter de Gruyter & Co., 1936), "Rerum Chalcedonensium Collectio Vaticana," p. 18.

[55] "Pascasinus et Lucensis uiri uenerabiles episcopi et Bonifatius presbyter uicarii sedis apostolicae per Pascasinum uenerabilem episcopum dixerunt: Ea quae concordantibus fratribus nostris Maximo uenerabili Antiochenae ecclesiae episcopo et sancto et uenerabili Juuenali Hierosolymitano episcopo bono pacis placuisse noscuntur, id est ut Antiochena ecclesia duas Fenices et Arabiam habeat, Hierosolymitana uero tres Palaestinas habeat, etiam nostrae humilitatis interlocutione firmentur, ut nulla in posterum super hoc negotio supra dictis ecclesiis controuersia relinquatur."—*loc. cit.*

the consent of all the bishops to the agreement;[56] fourth, the decree of the judges, who were high-ranking laymen assisting at the Council in the name of the Emperor.[57] This was to be the final disposition. The imperial rescripts which had been previously issued were cancelled by the order of the Emperor.[58] From that time, then, the Bishop of Jerusalem was counted among the patriarchs by the Greeks.[59]

A question may well be raised about the validity of these proceedings at the Council of Chalcedon inasmuch as the papal legates acted beyond their powers, as the Pope himself stated.[60] Pope Leo, indeed, did not directly annul the arrangements thus made concerning Jerusalem; however, he did annul them indirectly through his statement that anything that was not in agreement with the ruling made by the Fathers of the Council of Nicaea, would never be able to obtain the consent of the Apostolic See.[61] Nevertheless the institution of this new patriarchate was

[56] "Omnes uniuersi uenerabiles episcopi uociferati sunt, quorum nomina infra scripta sunt: Et nos haec ipsa dicimus et consentimus eis quae a patribus dicta sunt."—*ibid.*, p. 19.

[57] "Magnificentissimi et gloriosissimi judices dixerunt: Opus et hic factum est sanctae trinitatis et diui clementissimi nostri imperatoris propositionis, ut ea quae iurgantur, ab eis qui altercari poterant, uni consilio deciderentur uoluntatique. Ad concordiam igitur Maximi sancti episcopi Antiochensium et Iuuenalis sancti episcopi Hierosolymitani factus consensus, sicuti singulorum expositio, firma ex nostra sententia et decreto sanctae synodi in perpetuo tempore permanebit, id est ut Maximus quidem sanctus episcopus siue sancta Antiochiensium ciuitas duas Fenices et Arabiam sub potestate sua habeat, Iuuenalis uero sanctus episcopus Hierosolymitanus siue sancta ecclesia quae sub ipso est, tres Palaestinas sub potestate sua habebit, . . ."—*loc. cit.*

[58] ". . . sopitis secundum praeceptum diui et clementissimi nostri domni uniuersis praumaticis aliisue promeritis a partibus litteris diuinis et multae in eis adscriptae hac scilicet causa."—*loc. cit.*

[59] Bianchi, II, 681.

[60] St. Leo Magnus, *Ep. CXIX* (ad Maximum Antiochenum): ". . . ad hoc tantum ab apostolica sunt sede directi, ut excisis haeresibus catholicae essent fidei defensores."—Schwartz, *Concilium Universale Chalcedonense*, IV, 74; Jaffé, n. 495.

[61] St. Leo Magnus, *Ep. CXIX* (ad Maximum Antiochenum): "Si quid sane ab his fratribus quos ad sanctam synodum uice mea misi, praeter id quod ad causam fidei pertinebat, gestum esse perhibetur, nullius erit penitus

accepted among the Greeks, and so it was tolerated by the Holy See for the sake of peace.[62]

Fortescue (1874-1923) stated that since the time of the Council of Chalcedon (451) "Jerusalem has always been counted among the patriarchal sees as the smallest and last."[63]

ARTICLE 5. THE PATRIARCHATE OF CONSTANTINOPLE

The See of Constantinople was from its beginning a suffragan see of the Metropolitan of Heraclea.[64] In the year 324 the capital of the Empire was moved from Rome to Constantinople. As a result of this change the city and the Church of Constantinople acquired a position of greater honor.[65]

The I Council of Constantinople (381) recognized this increase of honor in a practical way by calling Constantinople the *nova Roma,* and by granting it second place among the most important bishoprics, a place preceded only by the Bishopric of Rome, the center from which the Pope ruled over the Church.[66]

Up until that time Alexandria had been the second see, and Antioch the third. Canon 3 of the I Council of Constantinople sought to change that order by according second place to the See of Constantinople. However, as the Popes refused to confirm this canon, the change in the hierarchy was not accomplished; Alexandria was still second, Antioch third.[67] Pope Gregory the

---

firmitatis, quia ad hoc tantum ab apostolica sunt sede directi, ut excisis haeresibus catholicae essent fidei defensores. Quidquid enim praeter speciales causas synodalium conciliorum ad examen episcopale defertur, potest aliquam diiudicandi habere rationem, si nihil de eo est a sanctis patribus apud Nicaeam definitum. Nam quod ab illorum regulis et constitutione discordat, apostolicae sedis numquam poterit obtinere consensum."—*loc. cit.*

[62] "Ma nulladimeno appresso i Greci ebbe vigore l'istituzione fatta nella narrata guisa di questo nuovo patriarcato, il quale poi dalla santa sede per ben della pace fu tollerato."—Bianchi, II, 682.

[63] Fortescue, "Patriarch and Patriarchate"—*Catholic Encyclopedia,* XI, 550.

[64] Thomassinus, Pars I, Lib. I, cap. 10, n. 1.

[65] Thomassinus, *loc. cit.*

[66] Canon 3: "Constantinopolitanus episcopus habeat priores honoris partes post Romanum episcopum, eo quod sit ipsa nova Roma."—Mansi, III, 559.

[67] Grisar referred to this canon in the following words: "The decrees of the Synod of 381 were never fully communicated to the Roman See by the

Great (590-604) explicitly stated that the Roman Church did not approve the canon.[68]

A question may be asked concerning the intention of the Council of Constantinople (381) in enacting canon 3. Did it intend to confer merely an honorary precedence, or did it intend to acknowledge some jurisdiction at the same time? Authors do not agree in giving an answer to this question.

Thus Pitra (1812-1889) stated that just as in canon 7 the I Council of Nicaea (325) recognized only a privilege of honor for the Bishop of Jerusalem, in like manner nothing more than this was conferred on the Bishop of Constantinople by canon 3 of the I Council of Constantinople (381).[69] Schroeder, agreeing with Pitra on this point, also maintained that canon 3 involved merely a primacy of honor second only to that of Rome.[70]

Greeks, and this for a very weighty reason. Among these decrees was one—the third on the list of canons—which they did not wish to force on Rome's notice. This, in an arbitrary and unfair manner, exalts the see of Constantinople at the expense of the two other principal sees of the East. . . . There can be no doubt that this (canon) would have been condemned in the West, but the Easterns, . . . disturbed the early order of precedence in the Church by trying to raise the hitherto unimportant bishopric of Constantinople above Alexandria and Antioch. . . ."—*History of Rome,* I, 336; cf. *supra,* p. 7, *infra,* p. 31.

[68] St. Gregorius Magnus, *Registrum Epistolarum,* Lib. VII, Ep. 31 (ad Eulogium Episcopum Alexandrinum et Anastasium episcopum Antiochenum): "Romana autem ecclesia eosdem canones vel gesta synodi illius hactenus non habet, nec accepit, in hoc autem eandem Synodum suscepit, quod est per eam contra Macedonium definitum."—*MGH, Gregorii I Papae Registrum Epistolarum,* Tomus I, pars II, p. 479; Jaffé, n. 1477.

[69] "Quemadmodum enim episcopo Hierosolymorum in canone VII nicaeno datum fuit solum honoris privilegium, similiter neque aliud episcopo byzantino, vi canonis (III) constantinopolitani, inditum est. . . ."—Pitra, *Iuris Ecclesiastici Graecorum Historia et Monumenta,* II, xliii.

[70] "So far as the phrase 'primacy of honor' is concerned, there is here no question of supremacy or ecclesiastical jurisdiction, though it was not so long afterward that he began to claim and to exercise such jurisdiction over the six provinces of Thrace, till then subject to Heraclea, and over the twenty-two provinces of Asia Minor and Pontus, originally subject to Ephesus and Caesarea. These rights of jurisdiction, though usurped, were confirmed by the Council of Chalcedon (451) in its famous 28th canon."—*General Councils,* p. 66.

Grisar, on the other hand, held that by canon 3 the I Council of Constantinople (381) intended to confer on the Bishop of Constantinople more than a mere honorary precedence, for he stated that "they also handed over to the control of the Bishop of Constantinople the whole diocese of Thrace, formerly governed by the Bishop of Heraclea."[71]

From both a legal and juridical point of view it makes little difference whether or not this canon was intended to grant jurisdiction to the Bishop of Constantinople. The canon was rejected by Rome, hence it was worthless as a law. In practice, however, even though there was no legal foundation to justify such actions, the Bishops of Constantinople, during the interval between the I Council of Constantinople (381) and the Council of Chalcedon (451), acted on many occasions as if they had obtained not merely a place of greater honor but also a grant of more extensive jurisdiction. Thus they usurped jurisdiction, and in so doing infringed on the rights of the Exarchs of Thrace, of Asia Prima, and of Pontus;[72] of the patriarchs of Antioch and Alexandria; and even on the patriarchal rights of the Bishop of Rome.

The following examples may be cited for the purpose of illustrating some ways in which this usurpation took place. Atticus, the Bishop of Constantinople (406-426), gave the episcopal see of Philippopolis in Thrace to Silvanus, and later transferred him to Troas in Hellespontine Phrygia. These acts contravened the rights of the Exarchs of Thrace and Asia, as did a law which Atticus obtained from Theodosius II, by which it was decreed that no

---

[71] *History of Rome,* I, 336.

[72] The word *exarch* is a title that became proper to the Bishops of Heraclea, Caesarea in Cappadocia, and Ephesus when the title *patriarch* was limited to the bishops of the major sees. These three exarchs, according to the common opinion, had a superior jurisdiction over all the provinces of their dioceses, i.e., over the dioceses of Thrace, of Pontus, and of Asia Prima respectively, which dioceses were coextensive with the civil dioceses of the same name. This jurisdiction was confirmed for them by canon 6 of the I Council of Nicaea (325), and was like that of the patriarchs. Their superiority was mentioned again in canon 2 of the I Council of Constantinople (381). But with the rise to power of Constantinople, which was from its beginning a suffragan see of Heraclea, the exarchs were little by little reduced in importance.—Kurtscheid, I, 120, 122, 124; cf. *supra,* pp. 6 et 7.

bishop be designated without the judgment and authority of the Council of Constantinople. Thomassinus (1619-1695) rightly remarked that the Bishops of Constantinople very often attacked the rights of the Exarchs of Thrace, of Pontus, and of Asia Prima. The dioceses of these Exarchs were of relatively small domain and easy of approach from Constantinople, and thus existed as targets readily vulnerable.[73]

Even the patriarchs of the larger dioceses did not escape the aggrandizement of the Bishops of Constantinople. Thus Nectarius, the Bishop of Constantinople from 381 to 397, presided at a synod held in Constantinople in 394, even though the Bishops of Alexandria and Antioch were in attendance. This same Nectarius settled a dispute concerning the metropolitan see of Bostra in Arabia, the settling of which dispute rightfully belonged to the competence of the Bishop of Antioch.[74]

From 379 onward the Bishop of Constantinople tried to extend his jurisdiction to Eastern Illyricum, which was part of the Western Patriachate. Thus he encroached on the patriarchal rights of the Bishop of Rome.

Illyricum prior to 379 was one of the prefectures of the Roman Empire. Its capital was Sirmium. But in 379 Illyricum was divided into Eastern and Western Illyricum. Eastern Illyricum, whose capital was now Thessalonica, was ceded by Gratian to the Eastern Emperor Theodosius; while Western Illyricum, with Sirmium as its capital, remained in the Western Empire as a part of the prefecture of Italy. Prior to this division the entire prefecture of Illyricum was part of the Roman Patriarchate. After the division the ecclesiastical arrangement was not changed, both Eastern and Western Illyricum still forming part of the Roman Patriarchate. However, the Bishops of Constantinople began to extend their jurisdiction to Eastern Illyricum. The Popes, therefore, as a means of better safeguarding their rights, gave the Metropolitan of Thessalonica the higher status of Vicar Apostolic.[75]

The Bishops of Constantinople, therefore, infringed on the rights of other bishops. Until the time of the Council of Chalcedon

---

[73] Thomassinus, Pars I, Lib. I, cap. 10, nn. 6 & 8.

[74] *Ibid.*, nn. 4 & 9; Mansi, III, 851-854.

[75] Kurtscheid, I, 126; cf. *supra*, p. 16.

(451) there was no ecclesiastical enactment on which to base claims to wider jurisdiction, except canon 3 of the I Council of Constantinople (381). But this canon, as has already been shown, was invalid.[76]

At Chalcedon (451), however, further concessions were made to the Bishops of Constantinople. In canon 9 the Council declared the See of Constantinople competent in the matter of settling controversies arising between the metropolitan of a province and some other bishop or cleric by giving the bishop or cleric the option of bringing the case either before the exarch of the diocese or before the Patriarch of Constantinople.[77] Canon 17 gave the same option to anyone who was injured by his own metropolitan. The injured party could bring the case either before the exarch of the diocese or before the Bishop of Constantinople.[78]

Thomassinus maintained that the concession made by canons 9 and 17 of the Council of Chalcedon amounted to the grant of a certain universal jurisdiction in the cases of metropolitans throughout the five major dioceses of the Eastern Empire. These dioceses were the Orient, with its capital at Antioch; Egypt, with its capital at Alexandria; Asia, with its capital at Ephesus; Thrace, with its

---

[76] Cf. *supra,* pp. 23 et 24, *infra,* p. 31.

[77] Canon 9: "Si quis clericus habet cum clerico litem aut negotium, proprium episcopum ne relinquat, et ad saecularia judicia ne excurrat: sed causam prius apud proprium episcopum agat: vel de episcopi sententia, apud eos quos utraque pars elegerit, judicium agitetur. Si quis autem praeter haec fecerit, canonicis poenis subjiciatur. Si clericus autem cum proprio vel etiam alio episcopo negotium aut litem habeat, a provinciae synodo judicetur. Si autem cum ipsius provinciae metropolitano episcopus vel clericus controversiam habeat, dioecesis exarchum adeat, vel imperialis urbis Constantinopolis thronum, et apud eum litiget."—Mansi, VII, 362.

[78] Canon 17: "Quae sunt in unaquaque provincia, rurales vicinasque parochias, firmas et inconcussas manere apud eos qui illas tenent episcopos: Et maxime si XXX annorum tempore eas sine vi detinentes administraverint. Si autem intra XXX annos fuit aliqua vel fuerit de iis controversia, licere iis qui injuriam sibi fieri dicunt, de iis litem movere apud synodum provinciae. Si quis autem injuria afficiatur a proprio metropolitano, apud exarchum dioecesis, vel Constantinopolitanam sedem litiget, sicut prius dictum est. Sin autem etiam civitas aliqua ab imperatoria auctoritate innovata est, vel deinceps innovata fuerit, civiles et publicas formas ecclesiasticarum quoque parochiarum ordo consequatur."—Mansi, VII, 366.

capital at Heraclea; and Pontus, with its capital at Caesarea in Cappadocia.[79] He also stated that the Bishops of Constantinople had used at times this *ius praeventionis* in the years before the Council of Chalcedon (451) with the consent of the parties.[80]

Pitra, on the contrary, held that the jurisdiction here referred to probably was intended to embrace only the patriarchate of Constantinople, and not those of Alexandria and Antioch. This he stated in his explanation of canons 9, 17, and 28 of the Council of Chalcedon.[81]

Pope Nicholas I (858-867), however, in a letter written in 865 to the Byzantine Emperor, Michael III (842-867), gave a different meaning for canon 9. He stated that cases of complaints of clerics or bishops against their metropolitans were, according to this canon, to be taken to the primate of the diocese for settlement, but if the cleric or bishop were in the neighborhood of Constantinople, and wished to be satisfied with the judgment of that Bishop,

---

[79] ". . . Canone hujus Concilii IX (Act. II) statutum est ut si Episcopo, si Clerico causa esset adversus Metropolitanum, fas esset eam referre ad judicium Exarchi, aut Archiepiscopi Constantinopolitani: . . . Eadem optandi, alternandique libertas rursus indulgetur Canone XVII. Id vero quid aliud erat, quam universalis quaedam jurisdictio in causas Metropolitanorum per quinque majores Orientalis Imperii Dioceses Constantinopolitano Episcopo accumulata?"—Thomassinus, Pars I, Lib. I, cap. 10, n. 12.

[80] ". . . Hoc ipso praeventionis jure aliquando usi fuerant Episcopi ante Constantinopolitani de partium consensu: exempla superius aliqua attigimus. . . ."—*loc. cit.*

[81] ". . . Manifestum vero erit tribus hisce novis chalcedonensium decretis crevisse vehementer sedem constantinopolitanam, multisque fuisse privilegiis exaltatam. Nono enim statuitur ut clericus qui cum metropolitano agit, provocet vel ad primatem sive exarchum, vel ad episcopum constantinopolitanum; id vero infra fines unius patriarchatus constantinopolitani constitisse ideo veri simile est, quod decretum nullum sive antiocheni sive alexandrini patriarchae memoriam habeat; quanto magis absurdum erit opinari aliquid de romano pontifice excogitatum ibi esse, quum in canone XXVIII secundum tantum gradus post sedem romanam, minime vero ac nullibi primus supremi iudicis locus tribuatur constantinopolitano. Nedum igitur huic detur metropolitanos omnes, caeteris patriarchis posthabitis, iudicare subiectos, immo tantum quibusnam limitibus contineatur novi patriarchae iurisdictio, aperte canone XXVIII declaratur, scilicet Ponto, Asia et Thracia, et si quae forte nova ecclesia inter gentes barbaras et hyperboraeas accreverit. . . ."—Pitra, *Iuris Ecclesiastici Graecorum Historia et Monumenta,* I, 535-536.

he could seek it.[82] The Pope stated that the canon distinguished between the precept or general rule of going to the primate and the permission or indult of going to the Bishop of Constantinople.[83] Finally, he interpreted the words *primatem dioeceseos* as if the word *dioeceseos* were plural instead of singular, and thus applied them to the Roman Pontiff.[84]

Cardinal Hergenröther (1824-1890) referred to this interpretation of Pope Nicholas. He stated that this was not the way that the Council of Chalcedon intended that the canon be interpreted; and he declared his belief that the canon referred only to the East.[85]

To the Bishop of Constantinople the Council of Chalcedon likewise acknowledged the right to ordain the metropolitans of the dioceses of Pontus, of Thrace, and of Asia, and also the bishops in the parts of these dioceses occupied by the barbarians.[86]

---

[82] Nicholas I, *Ep. 88* (ad Michalem Graecorum Imperatorem): ". . . In quo (canone IX Concilii Chalcedonensis) hic tenor observandus est, ut, si videlicet clericus aut episcopus adversus metropolitanum habet querelam et tanta urguetur [urgetur?] necessitate vel si hoc grave non ferat, ubicumque sit positus, primatem dioceseos petat; quodsi iuxta Constantinopolitanam urbem quisquam eorum constitutus et solius praesulis eius iudicio velit esse contentus, petat eandem regiam urbem. . . ."—*MGH,* Epistolarum, Tom. VI, *Epistolae Karolini Aevi,* IV, 471.

[83] ". . . Cum enim dixisset: *Petat primatem dioeceseos,* praeceptum posuit eadem sancta synodus regulamque constituit. Cum vero disiunctiva coniunctione addidisset: *Aut sedem regiae urbis Constantinopolitanae,* liquet profecto, quia hoc secundum permissionem indulsit. . . ."—*loc. cit.*

[84] ". . . Quem autem primatem dioeceseos sancta synodus dixerit praeter apostoli primi vicarium, nullus penitus intellegitur. . . ."—*loc. cit.*

[85] ". . . Der Papst erklärt den Canon sicher nicht richtig nach dem Sinne den man in Chalcedon intendirte . . . Sicher bezieht sich der Canon nur auf den Orient. . . ."—Hergenröther, *Photius, Patriarch von Constantinopel* (3 vols., Regensburg: 1867-1869), I, p. 568, footnote 92.

[86] Canon 28: "Sanctorum patrum decreta ubique sequentes, et canonem qui nuper lectus est, centum et quinquaginta Dei amantissimorum episcoporum agnoscentes, eadem quoque et nos decernimus ac statuimus de privilegiis sanctissimae ecclesiae Constantinopolis novae Romae. Etenim antiquae Romae Throno quod urbs illa imperaret, jure patres privilegia tribuerunt. Et eadem consideratione moti centum quinquaginta Dei amantissimi episcopi, sanctissimo novae Romae throno aequalia privilegia tribuerunt, recte judicantes, urbem quae et imperio et senatu honorata sit, et aequalibus cum antiquissima regina Roma privilegiis fruatur, etiam in rebus ecclesiasticis, non secus ac illam, extolli ac magnifieri, secundam post illam existentem:

The canon which contained this grant was enacted after the papal legates had departed from the assembly. On the next day, in session XVI, they demanded that the previous day's proceedings which had been transacted after their departure be read. They listened to the reading of the report, but strenuously objected to the innovation which favored the See of Constantinople, for they claimed that it ran counter to the ruling adopted in canon 6 of the I Council of Nicaea. They furthermore read a portion of their mandate from the Pope in order to evince the rightfulness of their opposition to the newly invoked innovation.[87]

The bishops who had favored the innovation on the previous day testified, on being questioned, that they had taken their action, not under duress, but freely. Among them Bishop Eusebius of Dorylaeum (in Phrygia) stated that he had read the contents of the canon to the Pope in Rome in the presence of clerics of Constantinople, and that the Pope had accepted the ruling. From this one can conclude that Eusebius either submitted a false statement of what had happened, or misrepresented the issue in his meeting with the Pope.[88] Eventually the judges ratified the new arrangement.[89] The bishops approved this decision of the judges,[90] but

---

ut et Ponticae et Asianae et Thraciae dioecesis metropolitani soli, praeterea episcopi praedicatarum diaecesum quae sunt inter barbaros, a praedicto throno sanctissimae Constantinopolitanae ecclesiae ordinentur: unoquoque scilicet praedictarum dioecesum metropolitano cum provinciae episcopis, provinciae episcopos ordinante, quemadmodum divinis canonibus est traditum. Ordinari autem, sicut dictum est, praedictarum dioecesum metropolitanos a Constantinopolitano archiepiscopo, convenientibus de more factis electionibus, et ad ipsum relatis."—Mansi, VII, 370.

[87] "Sanctorum quoque patrum constitutionem prolatam nulla patiamini temeritate violari vel imminui, servantes omnimodis personae nostrae in vobis (quos vice nostra transmisimus), dignitatem: ac si qui forte civitatum suarum splendore confisi, aliquid sibi tentaverint usupare, hoc qua dignum est constantia retundatis."—Mansi, VII, 443.

[88] "Eusebius episcopus Dorylaei dixit: Sponte subscripsi, quoniam et hanc regulam sanctissimo papae in urbe Roma ego relegi, praesentibus clericis Constantinopolitanis, eamque suscepit."—Mansi, VII, 450.

[89] "Gloriosissimi judices dixerunt: Ex his quae gesta sunt, et ab unoquoque deposita, perpendimus, omnem quidem primatum et honorem praecipuum secundum canones, antiquae Romae Dei amantissimo archiepiscopo conservari: oportere autem sanctissimum archiepiscopum regiae Constantinopolis

the papal legates remained firm in their opposition.[91]

In letters both to Anatolius, the Bishop of Constantinople (449-458), and to Marcianus and Pulcheria Augusta (450-457), Pope Leo I (440-461) expressed his mind on the subject. He expressed his sorrow and pain, in a letter to Anatolius, that the latter should try to infringe on the order ratified at the Council of Nicaea with reference to the major sees.[92] He stated that canon 3 of the Council of Constantinople (381), the canon that had been appealed to as an argument at the Council of Chalcedon in favor of the change, was never shown to the Popes by the Bishops of Constantinople. It, therefore, was never approved by the Popes. Accordingly it was invalid from the beginning and did not acquire validity simply with the passing of the years.[93]

In his letter to Pulcheria Augusta, the Pope again referred to the invalidity of canon 3 of the Council of Constantinople,[94] and

novae Romae eisdem primatibus honoris et ipsum dignum esse, et potestatem habere ordinare metropolitas in Asiana et Pontica et Thracia dioecesibus. . . ."—Mansi, VII, 451.

[90] "Reverendissimi episcopi clamaverunt: Haec justa sententia: haec omnes dicimus, haec omnibus placent. . . ."—Mansi, VII, 454.

[91] "Lucentius reverendissimus episcopus (vicarius sedis apostolicae) dixit: Sedes apostolica nobis praesentibus humiliari non debet: et ideo quaecumque in praejudicium canonum vel regularum hesterna die gesta sunt nobis absentibus, sublimitatem vestram petimus, ut circumduci jubeatis: sin alias, contradictio nostra his gestis inhaereat, ut noverimus quid apostolico viro universalis ecclesiae Papae referre debeamus: ut ipse aut de suae sedis injuria, aut de canonum eversione possit ferre sententiam."—Mansi, VII, 454.

[92] St. Leo Magnus, *Ep. CVI* (ad Anatolium Episcopum): "Doleo etiam in hoc dilectionem tuam esse prolapsam ut sacratissimas Nicaenorum canonum constitutiones conareris infringere, tamquam oportune se tibi hoc tempus optulerit, quo secundi honoris priuilegium sedes Alexandrina perdiderit et Antiochena Ecclesia proprietatem tertiae dignitatis amiserit, . . ."—Schwartz, *Concilium Universale Chalcedonense,* IV, 60; Jaffé, n. 483.

[93] St. Leo Magnus, *Ep. CVI* (ad Anatolium Episcopum): "Persuasioni enim tuae in nullo penitus suffragatur quorundam episcoporum ante sexaginta, ut jactas, annos facta conscriptio nec umquam a prodecessoribus tuis ad Apostolicae sedis missa notitiam, cui ab initio sui caducae dudumque conlapsae sera nunc et inutilia subicere fulcimenta uoluisti. . . ."—*ibid.,* p. 61; cf. *supra,* pp. 7 et 23-24.

[94] St. Leo Magnus, *Ep. CV* (ad Pulcheriam Augustam): "Superbum nimis est et immoderatum . . . ut uenerabilium patrum decreta soluantur, quorundam episcoporum proferre consensum, cui tot annorum series negauit effectum."—Schwartz, *Concilium Universale Chalcedonense,* IV, 58; Jaffé, n. 482.

he explicitly annulled the consent of the bishops on any matter opposed to the established ruling of the Council of Nicaea (325).[95]

The Bishop of Constantinople, therefore, met with resistance at Rome, since the Pope clearly refused to acknowledge to the Bishop of Constantinople a place of honor immediately after Rome, as canon 3 of the I Council of Constantinople had done, and also refused to acknowledge to the same Bishop the right of ordaining the metropolitans and some other bishops in the dioceses of Thrace, of Asia, and of Pontus, as canon 28 of the Council of Chalcedon (451) had done.

Canon 28 of Chalcedon as such has never been explicitly approved by the Church. Fortescue wrote that "the East, too, abandoned canon 28 till it was revived by Photius. It has never been included in any collection of canon law made by Catholics. As Orthodox canon law it dates, not from Chalcedon (451) but from their schism."[96] Schroeder stated that up to the IV Council of Constantinople (869-870) "canon 3 of the I Council of Constantinople (381) and canon 28 of Chalcedon (451) had been dead letters so far as Rome was concerned."[97]

The Bishops of Constantinople, however, continued to exercise, as a matter of fact, the jurisdiction confirmed for them by the invalid canon 28 of Chalcedon (451); indeed, they even tried to rule over the other major eastern Bishops of Alexandria, Antioch, and Jerusalem.[98]

In 545 Justinian stated, in one of his laws, that Constantinople had second place in the hierarchy,[99] and Pope Gregory the Great

[95] St. Leo Magnus, *Ep. CV* (ad Pulcheriam Augustam): "Consensiones vero episcoporum sanctorum canonum apud Nicaeam conditorum regulis repugnantes unita nobiscum uestrae fidei pietate in irritum mittimus et per auctoritatem beati Petri apostoli generali prorsus definitione cassamus. . . ." —*loc. cit.*

[96] Fortescue, *Lesser Eastern Churches* (London: Catholic Truth Society, 1913), p. 181, footnote.

[97] *General Councils*, p. 173.

[98] Kurtscheid, I, 121.

[99] "Ideoque sancimus secundum earum definitiones sanctissimum senioris Romae papam primum esse omnium sacerdotum, beatissimum autem archiepiscopum Constantinopoleos Novae Romae secundum habere locum post sanctam apostolicam sedem senioris Romae, aliis autem omnibus sedibus praeponatur."—*Corpus Iuris Civilis*, Vol. III, *Novellae* (131. 2).

(590-604) accommodated himself to the new order that was prescribed among the Greeks when, in 591, he addressed a letter to the four major eastern Bishops.[100]

The question may be asked whether St. Gregory intended to recognize Constantinople as the second see when he addressed his letter in this way? Grisar seems to think so.[101] In the opinion of the present writer, however, this change in rank was not intended by Pope Gregory. In proof of this one need only point to the replies given by Pope Nicholas I (858-867) in answer to the queries of the Bulgarians. In the 93rd response, the Pope definitely declared that Alexandria held second place among the Patriarchs. This response was given in the year 866.[102]

The first legal text which officially recognized Constantinople as the second see is to be found in canon 21 of the IV Council of Constantinople (869-870).[103]

As far as patriarchal jurisdiction is concerned, the Popes at first objected strenuously to this usurpation of power by the Bishops of Constantinople. Later on, although as far as the present writer knows there was no express grant of jurisdiction for the exercise of these rights, the Popes adopted a policy of silence.[104]

---

[100] St. Gregorius Magnus, *Registrum Epistolarum,* Lib. I, ep. 24: "Gregorius Johanni Constantinopolitano, Eulogio Alexandrino, Gregorio Antioceno, Johanni Hierosolimitano. . . ."—*MGH, Registrum Epistolarum Grcyorii I Papae,* Tom. I, p. 28; Jaffé, n. 1092.

[101] *History of Rome,* I, 337.

[102] *Ep. XCIX* (Responsa ad Consulta Bulgarorum), cap. 93: "Porro quis patriarcharum secundus sit a Romano, consulitis. Sex juxta quod sancta Romana tenet ecclesia et Niceni canones innuunt et sancti praesules Romanorum defendunt et ipsa ratio docet, Alexandrinus patriarcharum a Romano papa secundus est."—*MGH,* Epistolarum, Tom. VI, *Epistolae Karolini Aevi,* IV, 598; Jaffé, n. 2812. For a more complete analysis of the parts of this letter which pertain to patriarchs see chapter III of this work, pp. 59 ff.

[103] *Infra,* chapter IV, pp. 64 et 65.

[104] "During the Acacian schism (484-519), the patriarch Acacius and his successors consolidated their position in reference to the 28th canon of Chalcedon. Pope Hormisdas (514-523) and the Emperor Justin I (518-527) strove successfully for the reunion of the patriarch of Constantinople with Rome; their efforts were crowned with success in 519. Eight years later Justinian

But at the IV Council of Constantinople reference was made in canon 17 to the ancient custom confirmed in the I Council of Nicaea (325) for Alexandria, a custom by which the Bishop of Alexandria had authority over the Egyptian provinces. The Council of Constantinople then decreed that this *prisca consuetudo* be conserved in all things in Old Rome, in New Rome, in Antioch, and in Jerusalem, in such a way that the Bishops of these sees have power of convoking in synod, when necessity urged, the metropolitans whom they ordained or to whom they gave the pallium; and also of coercing and correcting these metropolitans when they were perhaps accused of certain crimes. This *prisca consuetudo,* therefore, referred to by the Council of Constantinople was the patriarchal rank. And so in this canon one finds the first explicit grant of patriarchal rank to the Bishop of Constantinople. Here he explicitly was given patriarchal jurisdiction, although the powers granted by canons 9 and 17 of the Council of Chalcedon (451) may also be looked upon as containing a grant of some patriarchal privileges in judicial matters.

It seems to the present writer that for some time even before the IV Council of Constantinople (869-870) the Bishops of Constantinople did enjoy patriarchal jurisdiction by reason of tacit papal approval of their acts.[105]

Referring to the rise of Constantinople to a higher place in the hierarchy, Fortescue (1874-1923), in his article "Patriarch and Patriarchate" in the *Catholic Encyclopedia,* wrote:

> Pope Leo I (440-461) refused to admit this canon (c. 28 of Chalcedon), which was made in the absence of his legates; for centuries Rome still refused to give the second place to Constantinople. It was not until the IV Lateran Council (1215) that the Latin Patriarch of Con-

---

became Emperor (527-565), and there is no further protest on the part of the Popes regarding the position of Constantinople as one of the eastern patriarchates. . . ."—Eidenschink, *The Election of Bishops in the Letters of Gregory the Great,* The Catholic University of America Canon Law Studies, n. 215 (Washington, D. C.: The Catholic University of America Press, 1945), p. 5 (hereinafter cited as Eidenschink); cf. *infra,* pp. 60 et 61.

[105] Cf. *infra,* pp. 60-62; 68-69; where these points will be more fully treated.

stantinople was allowed this place; in 1439 the Council of Florence gave it to the Greek Patriarch. Nevertheless in the East, the Emperor's wish was powerful enough to obtain recognition for his patriarch; from Chalcedon we must count Constantinople as practically, if not legally, the second Patriarchate.[106]

[106] *Catholic Encyclopedia,* XI, 550.

CHAPTER II

THE PATRIARCHAL JURISDICTION IN ANTIQUITY

ARTICLE 1. THE NATURE OF ECCLESIASTICAL POWER IN GENERAL

The Church as founded by Jesus Christ exists as a hierarchical society. Its members do not reflect a common equality in rank. Its body of sacred government is constituted by higher ranking members. Generically the term "hierarchy" designates a power of rule which is exercised by these higher ranking members within a framework of subalternated authorities, all of whom acknowledge the Bishop of Rome as possessing the primatial authority in the Church.[1]

The hierarchy or sacred authority in the Church is differentiated by reason of its object and by reason of its origin. Thus one speaks of the *hierarchy of jurisdiction* and the *hierarchy of orders* as differentiated from each other from the viewpoint of its object. And one refers to the *divine hierarchy* and the *ecclesiastical hierarchy* as differentiated in their origin. The hierarchy of orders implies the exercise of spiritual power for the purpose of sanctifying the faithful through the production and the administration of the sacraments, while the hierarchy of jurisdiction connotes the exercise of a spiritual power for the purpose of teaching and ruling men with a view to directing them to life's ultimate purpose. The divine hierarchy derives its existence and character through the immediate and positive institution of it by Christ, whereas the ecclesiastical hierarchy does so through the immediate and positive institution of it by the Church.[2]

---

[1] "In genere, hierarchia designat principatum qui a personis sibi invicem subordinatis exercetur."—Tanquerey, *Synopsis Theologiae Dogmaticae* (24. ed., 3 vols., recognita a J. Bord, Parisiis-Tornaci-Romae: Desclée et Socii, 1933-1938), I, 432 (hereinafter referred to as *Synopsis*).

[2] "Ratione objecti, hierarchia distinguitur duplex, *ordinis* scilicet et *jurisdictionis*. Prior exercet spiritualem potestatem ad fideles sanctificandos per sacramentorum confectionem et administrationem. Posterior ordinatur ad

In the divine hierarchy of orders and with regard to the valid exercise of these orders, all consecrated bishops are equal, all having the power of episcopal orders equally with the Roman Pontiff. Since, therefore, in the hierarchy of orders they are not constituted in diverse and substantially distinct grades, any gradation which may have existed or now exists among them must be sought either in the lawful use of the power of orders, or in their power of jurisdiction.[3]

In the divine hierarchy of jurisdiction, however, there are only two grades, the primacy of jurisdiction of Peter and his successors over the entire Church, and the jurisdiction of the subordinate episcopate, as is evident from the statement of canon 108, § 3, just quoted.

The Roman Pontiffs alone as the successors of Peter hold from divine law a superior jurisdiction. They enjoy full and supreme jurisdiction over the entire Church.[4] Bishops other than the Roman Pontiff are, therefore, equal as regards their episcopal jurisdiction, and this equality arises from the divine law.[5]

---

homines docendos et regendos in ordine ad aeternam salutem. Ratione originis, hierarchia est vel *divina,* vel *ecclesiastica,* prout procedit ex immediata et positiva institutione Christi vel Ecclesiae."—Tanquerey, *Synopsis* I, 432-433; "Ex divina institutione sacra hierarchia ratione ordinis constat Episcopis, presbyteris et ministris: ratione iurisdictionis, pontificatu supremo et episcopatu subordinato: ex Ecclesiae autem institutione alii quoque gradus accessere."—Canon 108, § 3.

[3] Wernz-Vidal, II, 637.

[4] Pope Damasus: ". . . sancta . . . Romana Ecclesia . . . evangelica voce Domini, et Salvatoris nostri primatum obtinuit: 'Tu es Petrus' inquientis, 'et super hanc petram aedificabo Ecclesiam meam: . . .' "—Mansi, VIII, 158, cf. *supra,* pp. 6-7, footnote; Concilium Vaticanum: ". . . quicunque in hac cathedra Petro succedit, is secundum Christi ipsius institutionem primatum Petri in universam Ecclesiam obtinet. . . ."—Denzinger, Bannwart, Umberg, *Enchiridion Symbolorum Definitionum et Declarationum de Rebus Fidei et Morum* (21.-23. ed., *Friburgi Brisgoviae:* Herder, 1937), n. 1824 (hereinafter cited as *Enchiridion*); "Romanus Pontifex, Beati Petri in primatu Successor, habet non solum primatum honoris, sed supremam et plenam potestatem iurisdictionis in universam Ecclesiam tum in rebus quae ad fidem et mores, tum in iis quae ad disciplinam et regimen Ecclesiae per totum orbem diffusae pertinent."—Can. 218, § 1. Cf. Tanquerey, *Synopsis,* I, 490.

[5] Wernz-Vidal, II, 638.

ARTICLE 2. THE NATURE OF PATRIARCHAL POWER

Since in the divine hierarchy of jurisdiction there are only two grades; namely, that of the Roman Pontiff and that of the ordinary bishops, the intermediate grades existing in the hierarchy between the Pope and the bishops belong, not to the divine hierarchy, but to the ecclesiastical hierarchy, of jurisdiction. That is to say, patriarchs, primates, exarchs, and metropolitans, in having a superior jurisdiction over ordinary bishops, have this not from divine law but only from ecclesiastical law. Theirs is a certain participation in the jurisdiction of the Roman Pontiff, either expressly or tacitly granted by him; and so it must naturally remain subject to the Roman Pontiff, who is free to transfer, to alter, indeed even to suppress these offices if he sees fit.[6]

Patriarchal jurisdiction, having always been a participation in the jurisdiction of the Roman Pontiff, was a derived jurisdiction. But jurisdiction could be derived from another in one of two possible ways: either it was perpetually attached by law to an office which one obtained, and then it was ordinary jurisdiction; or it was committed directly to its recipient, in which case it was delegated jurisdiction.[7] Patriarchal jurisdiction was permanently attached by law to the episcopal sees which held the patriarchal rank. It was, therefore, ordinary jurisdiction.[8]

That this jurisdiction was permanently attached to the patriarchal sees, and not committed personally to each individual incumbent nor made to depend on the merits of the bishops of these sees, is clearly stated by Pope Leo I (440-461) in a letter to Maximus, the Bishop of Antioch. In this letter the Pope stated that he held such a reverence for the canons of the I Council of Nicaea (325), that he would not permit them to be violated in favor of

---

[6] Wernz-Vidal, II, 637-639; cf. can. 109.

[7] "Potestas iurisdictionis ordinaria ea est quae ipso iure adnexa est officio: delegata, quae commissa est personae."—Can. 197, § 1; cf. Wernz-Vidal, II, 638; cf. Vermeersch-Creusen, *Epitome Iuris Canonici* (6. ed., 3 vols., Mechliniae-Romae: H. Dessain, 1937-1946), I, 259 ff. The notions of ordinary and of delegated power have ever been identical with the same notions as now defined in the law.

[8] Wernz-Vidal, II, 638.

something new. He then added that although the merits of Bishops sometimes differ, the rights of the sees remain.[9]

ARTICLE 3. LEGAL RIGHTS INCLUDED IN THE PATRIARCHAL POWER OF THE THREE EARLIEST PATRIARCHATES

The purpose of the present article is to show what legal rights were included in the jurisdiction possessed by the Bishops of Rome, of Alexandria, and of Antioch as Patriarchs. First of all it will be necessary to point out certain powers which these Patriarchs possessed otherwise than in virtue of their patriarchal rank. The Patriarchs of Alexandria and Antioch were also Bishops, and so they possessed the jurisdiction of the episcopacy; both were metropolitans, and therefore they also possessed the jurisdiction of metropolitans over their particular province. The Bishop of Rome, over and above these powers, enjoyed the primacy of jurisdiction over the entire Church. He, therefore, was the Bishop of Rome, the Metropolitan of his Italian province, the Patriarch of all the West, and the Supreme Pontiff of the universal Church.

"On account of his primacy, the patriarchal power of the Roman Pontiff more often was not clearly distinguished from it."[10]

In this article, then, the writer proposes to consider *ex professo* the rights which these three bishops enjoyed as patriarchs, in abstraction from the jurisdiction they possessed through other titles, except in so far as special mention of this may be necessary by reason of its connection with the patriarchal jurisdiction.

In the first place it will be necessary to point out, with Kurtscheid, that the "rights of patriarchs were not everywhere equal," and also that the Roman Pontiff did not exercise his patriarchal rights in all parts of the West in the same way as the patriarchs of the East exercised the patriarchal rights in their territories.[11]

---

[9] *Ep. 119* (ad Maximum Antiochenum Episcopum: ". . . diuersa nonnumquam sunt merita praesulum, iura tamen permanent sedium, quibus possunt aemuli perturbationem aliquam fortassis inferre, non tamen possunt minuere dignitatem. . . ."—Schwartz, *Concilium Universale Chalcedonense,* IV, 74.

[10] Kurtscheid, I, 124; cf. also, Wernz-Vidal, II, 641-642; Grisar, *History of Rome,* I, 342-343-344; cf. *infra,* pp. 53 ff.

[11] Kurtscheid, I, 122-123.

Because of this fact, the question will be treated in three sections, the first dealing with the patriarchate of Antioch, the second with that of Alexandria, and the third with that of Rome. In each of these sections those ancient patriarchal rights which the present writer has been able to discover will be treated.

Section 1. The Patriarchate of Antioch

In this section the jurisdictional rights which were enjoyed by the patriarchal Bishop of Antioch in the early ages of the Church will be shown from ancient writings. These rights will be treated separately under the following headings: A) The right of the patriarch to ordain metropolitans and to consent to the ordination of bishops; B) The patriarchal right of supervision over the entire patriarchate; C) Rights pertaining to patriarchal synods.

A) The Right of the Patriarch to Ordain Metropolitans and to Consent to the Ordination of Bishops

When the Council of Nicaea (325) recognized and confirmed the superior rank of the see of Antioch in canon 6, the Bishop of Antioch already enjoyed the right of ordaining the metropolitans of the provinces of his diocese.[12] That he enjoyed this right of ordaining the metropolitans in that territory is evident from a letter of Pope Innocent I (401-417) to Alexander (413-c.420), a Bishop of Antioch. In this letter the Pope said that the Bishop of Antioch had a singular authority in regard to the ordination of metropolitans.[13]

Since no evidence can be found that this right was conferred on the Bishop of Antioch by any Pope between the time of the I Council of Nicaea (325) and the time of this letter, one may conclude that it was enjoyed by that Bishop at the time of the Council and even before. This conclusion is given added weight by the fact

---

[12] *Supra*, pp. 17 ff.

[13] St. Innocentius I, *Ep. XXIV* (ad Alexandrum Antiochiae Episcopum): "Revolventes itaque auctoritatem Nicaenae Synodi, . . . de Antiochena ecclesia . . . super dioecesim suam praedictam ecclesiam, non super aliquam provinciam recognoscimus constitutam. . . . Itaque arbitramur, frater charissime, ut sicut metropolitanos auctoritate ordinas singulari, sic. . . ."—*MPL,* XX, 547, 548; Jaffé, n. 310.

that a superior position, then already existing, was confirmed for the Bishop of Antioch by the Council in 325.

Concerning the other Bishops of these provinces, the Pope further stated that the Bishop of Antioch was not to permit their elevation without his permission.[14]

The Pope, therefore, declared that the elevation of these other bishops was a matter of conscience for the Bishop of Antioch, but he did not insist that these bishops be personally ordained by the Bishop of Antioch. For in giving the rules as to how this latter Bishop was to exercise his supervision, he told him that those who were far distant from him he could order to be ordained by those who currently ordained them on their own authority. Their ordination was not to take place, however, without the proper letter of permission. Those who resided close by he could order to come to him for ordination if he felt that this should be done.[15]

Kurtscheid stated that Pope Innocent I, by pointing to the Council of Nicaea (325), confirmed the right of the Patriarch to ordain the metropolitans of the entire region and of *consenting* to the ordination of bishops.[16]

Hefele, in his explanation of the canons of Nicaea (325), treated of the nature of the rights of the metropolitan of Antioch. He declared that the Bishop ordained the metropolitans and *confirmed* the ordination of simple bishops who could be ordained by their immediate metropolitans.[17]

---

[14] "Itaque arbitramur ut sicut metropolitanos auctoritate ordinas singulari, sic et caeteros non sine permissu conscientiaque tua sinas episcopos procreari."—*ibid.*, p. 548.

[15] "In quibus hunc modum recte servabis, ut longe positos litteris datis ordinari censeas ab his, qui nunc eos suo tantum ordinant arbitratu; vicinos autem, si aestimas, ad manus impositionem tuae gratiae statuas pervenire."—*loc. cit.*

[16] "Innocentius I anno 415 allegans concilium Nicaenum confirmat ius patriarchae ordinandi metropolitas totius territorii et praestandi consensum pro ordinatione episcoporum (Coustant 850)"—Kurtscheid, I, 121. In listing the rights of patriarchs in general, Kurtscheid included: "Jus consecrandi metropolitas territorii et praestandi consensum ad episcoporum ordinationem, nisi haec quoque, sicut Alexandriae, patriarchae erat reservata."—*ibid.*, p. 122.

[17] ". . . la nature des droits du métropolitan d'Antioche: a) il ordonnait les métropolitains; b) il confirmait l'ordination des simples évêques, laquelle pouvait être faite par les métropolitains immédiates."—Hefele-Leclercq, *Histoire des Conciles,* I, 560.

However, it seems that the letter of Pope Innocent I referred to something more than a mere confirmation of a past act. It seemed to refer to a definite power over future acts, for it stated: . . . *arbitramur . . . ut . . . caeteros non sine permissu conscientiaque tua sinas episcopos procreari.* This view seems to be demanded also by the next sentence of the letter in which the Pope gave detailed instructions as to how this supervision was to be exercised. There one finds a distinction made between bishops residing afar off—*longe positos*—and those dwelling near-by—*vicinos.* The former could be commanded by the Bishop of Antioch to receive their ordination—*censeas ordinari*—from those who currently ordained them, but with this difference. Currently they ordained them without consulting Antioch—*suo tantum arbitratu;* thenceforward they were to ordain them only after a letter had been granted—*litteris datis*—that is, *non sine permissu conscientiaque* (*episcopi Antiochiae*). Those who dwelled near-by (*vicinos*) could be commanded by the Bishop of Antioch to present themselves to him for ordination.

The tenor of the entire passage, therefore, seems to indicate, in the opinion of the present writer, that the Bishop of Antioch had more than the mere power of confirming bishops already elected and consecrated; he had a power of veto in virtue of which he could forbid ordination, and thus render it unlawful for anyone to receive ordination, except from the Bishop of Rome; and for any Bishop, except the Bishop of Rome, to grant it.

B) The Patriarchal Right of Supervision Over the Entire Patriarchate

Canon 6 of the I Council of Nicaea (325) confirmed an ancient custom in virtue of which the Bishop of Antioch had a right of supervision over his patriarchal territory.[18]

As a consequence of this privilege he was to watch over the faith in his patriarchal diocese and protect it from heresy. Pope Leo I (440-461), in a letter written in 453, exhorted Maximus (449-455?), the Bishop of Antioch, to exercise this care. In this letter the Pope told him not to permit heretics to resist the gospel, and

[18] *Supra,* p. 3.

also not to permit the teachings of Nestorius or Eutyches to be defended by anyone. Maximus was told to exercise this vigilance "in orientalibus ecclesiis," and especially in those which the Council of Nicaea (325) had recognized as subject to the see of Antioch.[19] The Pope stated that it was fitting for Maximus to exercise the greatest watchfulness to prevent the spread of heresy.[20]

Moroni (1802-1883), in listing the jurisdictional rights of patriarchs, stated that they enjoyed the right of exercising a general inspection over all the ecclesiastical provinces depending on them.[21] However, he did not expressly indicate in this place any specific period of time to which his statement referred.

Kurtscheid, in treating of the law of the canons from the IV to the VII century, furnished a list of the patriarchal rights. In this list he stated that they enjoyed a right of vigilance over the observance of the laws of the Church in their entire territory.[22]

C) The Rights Pertaining to Patriarchal Synods

The Bishop of Antioch, by reason of his superior jurisdiction over all the provinces of his diocese, had the right to convoke in synod all the metropolitans and bishops of these provinces.

---

[19] Leo I, *Ep. 119* (ad Maximum Antiochenum Episcopum): ". . . neque ullo modo sinas in Orientalibus Ecclesiis maximeque his quas Antiochenae sedi sacratissimorum patrum Nicaeni canones deputarunt, ab improbis haereticis euangelio resultari et uel Nestorii uel Eutychis a quoquam dogma defendi, . . ."—Schwartz, *Concilium Universale Chalcedonense,* IV, 73; Jaffé, n. 495.

[20] ". . . Summa itaque uigilantia cautum esse te conuenit ne quid sibi haeretica prauitas audeat uindicare, cum te deceat his sacerdotali auctoritate resistere nosque saepius de profectu ecclesiarum tuis relationibus quid agatur, instruere. Dignum est enim te apostolicae sedis in hac sollicitudine esse consortem et ad agendi fiduciam priuilegia tertiae sedis agnoscere, quae in nullo cujusquam ambitione minuentur, . . ."—*loc. cit.*

[21] "I patriarchi di giurisdizione hanno . . . il diritto di avere una ispezione generale sopra tutte le provincie ecclesiastiche che ne dipendono."—Moroni, *Dizionario di Erudizione Storico-Ecclesiastica da S. Pietro sino ai Nostri Giorni* (103 vols. et 6 vols. Indicis, Venezia: 1840-1879), LI, 295 (hereinafter referred to as *Dizionario*).

[22] "Jura patriarcharum, licet non ubique aequalia fuerint, haec notantur: Jus vigilandi ut leges ecclesiasticae in universo territorio sibi commisso serventur, . . ."—Kurtscheid, I, 122.

The I Council of Nicaea (325) decreed in canon 5 that two synods be held every year in each province, one before lent, the other in the autumn.[23]

Since the metropolitan of the province held a place of superior jurisdiction over the other bishops of the province, the actual convocation of these synods as well as the duty of presiding at them devolved upon him.

In the aforementioned canon of Nicaea (325), the almost exclusive purpose of these synods seemed to look to the investigation of cases of alleged unjust excommunication. However, as Schroeder pointed out, the I Council of Constantinople (381) in canon 2 "rightly interprets this Nicene decree when it extends the duty of a provincial synod to an examination of the affairs of the entire province."[24]

The power of the metropolitans in regard to provincial synods was somewhat similar to the power exercised, at least from the fourth century, by the eastern patriarchs in regard to the patriarchal synods.

Kurtscheid, speaking of the eastern sees, stated that from the IV century the major cases, especially those concerning the faith, were usually treated in a synod attended by a greater number of bishops, very often of the entire patriarchate.[25] He listed two ex-

[23] Canon 5: "De excommunicatis. De his qui excommunicantur, siue de clero sint siue de laico agmine, ab episcopis per singulas prouincias, obtineat sententia iuxta canonem eos qui ab aliis abiciuntur ab aliis non recipiendos. Requiratur autem ne pussillanimitate aut pertinacia aut aliqua alia episcopi molestia excommunicati sunt. Ut ergo hoc decentius inquiratur, bene haberi placuit singulis annis per singulas prouincias bis in anno concilia fieri: ut omnibus simul episcopis in unum congregatis tales questiones inquirantur, et ita qui manifeste offenderunt episcopum rationabiliter excommunicati apud omnes esse putentur, quamdiu aut in communi aut episcopo placeat humaniorem pro his ferre sententiam. Concilia autem fiant, unum quidem ante quadragensimam ut omni pusillanimitate sublata munus mundum offeratur Deo, secundum autem circa tempus autumni."—Turner, *Ecclesiae Occidentalis Monumenta,* fasciculus primus, pars altera, p. 118.

[24] Schroeder, *General Councils,* p. 29; Concilium Constantinopolitanum I (381) canon 2: ". . . Servato autem praescripto de dioecesibus canone, clarum est quod unamquamque provinciam provinciae synodus administravit secundum ea quae fuerunt Nicaeae definita."—Mansi, III, 559.

[25] "A saeculo IV in Oriente de causis maioribus, praesertim fidei a maiore quoque episcoporum numero, plerumque totius patriarchatus, in synodo congregato tractari solebat."—Kurtscheid, I, 143.

amples of such synods, the one held at Antioch in 445, and the other held in the same city in 447.

Concerning patriarchal synods, he noted that they were not held at determined times, but only as necessity demanded; they were neither numerous, nor were disciplinary laws enacted at them except on rare occasions; the patriarch usually presided, the other bishops or their delegates also having a decisive vote.[26]

Theodoretus (ca. 420-458), Bishop of Cyrus in Syria—a see in the province of the Euphrates in the patriarchate of Antioch—in his letter to the Consul Nomus, written in 445, stated that he went to Antioch, not of his own accord, but because he was called five or six times to synods there, and obeyed these calls with difficulty. He went on to state that he attended in compliance with the ecclesiastical canon which considered one a criminal for refusing to attend a synod after having been summoned.[27]

Section 2. The Patriarchate of Alexandria

In this section the writer proposes to show, both from the sources and other early testimony, the jurisdictional rights which the patriarchal Bishop of Alexandria enjoyed in the early centuries. These rights may be listed as follows: A) The right of the Patriarch over the ordination of metropolitans and bishops; B) The right of the Patriarch over the transfer of bishops; C) The patriarchal right of supervision over the entire patriarchate; D) The rights pertaining to patriarchal synods; E) The patriarchal power relative to absolution from excommunication.

A) The Right of the Patriarch Over the Ordination of Metropolitans and Bishops

The Bishop of Alexandria had the right to ordain all the metropolitans who were subject to him. The letter of Pope Innocent I

---

[26] "Locum habebant non determinatis temporibus, sed prout necessitas id postularet. . . . Quare synodi patriarchales in sensu stricto non sunt numerosae et raro in eis leges disciplinares latae sunt. Praesidere solebat patriarcha, votum decisivum habebant tantum episcopi vel eorum delegati."—*loc. cit.*

[27] Theodoretus, *Ep. 81*: ". . . Noverit enim magnitudo tua, me nec . . . sponte mea intrasse Antiochiam, sed quinquies ac sexies vocatum vix paruisse. Parebam autem ut ecclesiastico canoni obsequerer, qui reum haberi jubet eum qui ad synodum vocatus adesse noluerit. . . ."—*MPG,* LXXXIII, 1262.

recognized this right as one enjoyed by the Bishop of Antioch.[28] But since the Bishop of Alexandria held in Egypt a position similar to that held in the diocese of the East by the Bishop of Antioch, it must be said that the latter too enjoyed this right of ordaining his subordinate metropolitans, even though one must recognize that the rights of these over-metropolitan or patriarchal bishops were not everywhere the same.

Hefele, in his commentary on canon 6 of the I Council of Nicaea (325), referred to the nature of the rights of the Patriarch of Alexandria, and expressly stated that the Bishop used to ordain the metropolitans who were subject to him.[29]

The right of ordination enjoyed by the Bishop of Alexandria was amplified by some of the authors. They claimed that he had the right of ordaining all the other bishops of the provinces within his jurisdiction. This was the opinion of Hefele, Kurtscheid, and Wernz (1842-1914)-Vidal (1868-1939).[30] However, Petavius (1583-1652) took the opposite view. He stated explicitly his belief that it was not necessary for all the bishops of the patriarchate to receive their ordination at Alexandria.[31]

B) The Right of the Patriarch Over the Transfer of Bishops

Considering the superior authority of the Bishop of Alexandria in accordance with which he may have enjoyed the special right of consecrating all the Bishops within his jurisdiction, one may rightly inquire about his power over them after their consecration had taken place, and ask if perchance he enjoyed any right of transferring them from one see to another within his patriarchate.

Before giving a definite answer to this question, one must simultaneously admit to the fact that according to the general norms of ecclesiastical discipline in the early fourth century the transfer of a bishop from one see to another was forbidden. The first known conciliar law that forbade this was canon 15 of the I Council of Nicaea (325).[32]

---

[28] *Supra*, p. 40.

[29] *Histoire des Conciles*, I, 558.

[30] *Histoire des Conciles*, I, 558; Kurtscheid, I, 122; Wernz-Vidal, II, 652.

[31] *Notae Petavii—MPG*, LXVI, 1415.

[32] Canon 15: "De clericis ne de ciuitate ad aliam transeant. Propter grandem tumultum et seditiones quae factae sunt placuit omnimodis auferri

Schroeder stated that "it is difficult to say to what canon the council here alludes, if indeed the allusion is to any canon properly so called. It is not improbable that the rule invoked had its basis in a custom that went back to Apostolic times."[33]

This prohibition was renewed in canon 21 of the Council of Antioch (341),[34] and again in canons 1 and 3 of the Council of Sardica (343).[35]

The prohibition of the transfer of a bishop from one bishopric to another was not, however, an absolute one, and so it was possible to obtain a dispensation from it.[36] The *Canones Apostolorum* stated that the general law could be dispensed with for a reasonable cause;[37] and Schroeder related that "the Church soon found it necessary to make exceptions to the rule, and it was not long before

---

consuetudinem quae est contra canonem, si inuenti fuerint in aliquibus partibus de ciuitate ad ciuitatem migrantes, nec episcopo nec praesbitero neque diacono liceat. Si quis autem post sancti et magni concilii definitionem tale aliquid adtemptaverit aut sese dederit negotio, cassabitur omnimodo hujusmodi machinatio et restituetur aecclesiae in qua aut episcopus aut praesbiter aut diaconus fuerit ordinatus."—Turner, *Ecclesiae Occidentalis Monumenta,* fasciculus primus, pars altera, p. 134.

[33] *General Councils,* pp. 44-45.

[34] Canon 21: "Episcopus ab alia paroecia nequaquam migret ad aliam, nec sponte sua prorsus insiliens nec vi coactus a populis nec ab episcopis necessitate conpulsus; maneat autem in aecclesia quam primitus a Deo sortitus est nec inde transmigret, secundum pristinum de hac re iam terminum constitutum."—Turner, *Ecclesiae Occidentalis Monumenta,* Tomus Secundus, pars secunda, p. 295.

[35] Canon 1: "Non magis mala consuetudo quam perniciosa corruptela funditus eradicanda est, ne cui liceat episcopo de ciuitate sua ad aliam ciuitatem transire. . . ."—Turner, *Ecclesiae Occidentalis Monumenta,* Tomus Prior, Fasciculus Alter, Pars Tertia, p. 490; Canon 3: "Illud quoque, ut episcopus de provincia ad aliam provinciam in qua sunt episcopi non transeat; nisi forte a fratribus suis inuitatus, ne uideamur ianuam caritatis clausisse."—*ibid.,* p. 492.

[36] Kurtscheid, I, 115.

[37] Canon 14: "Episcopo non licere alienam paroeciam propria relicta peruadere, licet cogatur a plurimis, nisi forte quis eum rationabilis causa compellat tamquam qui possit ibidem constitutis plus lucri conferre et in causa religionis aliquid profecto prospicere. Et hoc non a semetipso pertemtet, sed multorum episcoporum iudicio et maxima supplicatione perficiat."—Turner, *Ecclesiae Occidentalis Monumenta,* fasciculus primus, pars prior, p. 14.

these multiplied to such an extent that Gregory of Nazianzus in 382 spoke of the prohibition as no longer existent. In the Western Church it was more strictly observed."[38]

Keeping these regulations in mind, one may state that the Bishop of Alexandria could dispense from this law and transfer bishops within his patriarchate when such a transfer was necessary for the good of the Church.

Using this power, Bishop St. Athanasius (328-373) transferred Siderius, the Bishop of Palaebisca, a village of Pentapolis, to the Church of Ptolemais in Pentapolis. The transfer was made because it was necessary that the spark of true faith be enkindled more and more in that place; and so Athanasius, recognizing in Siderius a capacity for greater undertakings, ordered him to go to Ptolemais and govern the Church there.

This information concerning St. Athanasius in transferring one of the suffragan bishops of his patriarchate to another see comes to us from Synesius, a Bishop of Ptolemais, who related it in his letter to Theophilus (385-412), the Bishop of Alexandria.[39]

Synesius did not state in his letter whether Athanasius in making this transfer acted independently or in synod. However, Wernz-Vidal stated that there is no conclusive proof that patriarchs, acting independently of the synod, had the right of transferring the Archbishops or Bishops of their patriarchate;[40] and Kurtscheid, after listing a number of cases in which a dispensation was granted and the transfer of a Bishop was made, including the case of Siderius, stated that in all of them the transfer was made with the consent of the Bishops of a synod, who thought that the rigor of the law had to be mitigated for a needed correspondence to the utility of the Church.[41] Indeed, canon 14 of the *Canones Apostolorum* explicitly stated that the transfer was to be made only on the judgment of many bishops.[42]

---

[38] *General Councils,* 45-46.

[39] Synesius, *Ep. LXVII* (Theophilo Alexandrino): ". . . Athanasium . . . cum exiguam adhuc orthodoxae fidei scintillam, quae in Ptolemaide erat, fovere, et magis magisque oporteret accendere, hominem illum (Siderium) majoribus rebus gerendis idoneum eo commigrare jussisse, ut . . . Ecclesiam gubernaret."—*MPG,* LXVI, 1418.

[40] Wernz-Vidal, II, 652, footnote 108.

[41] Kurtscheid, I, 115.

[42] Cf. *supra,* p. 47.

C) The Patriarchal Right of Supervision Over the Entire Patriarchate

The Bishop of Alexandria had a general right of supervision over his entire patriarchate. This pertained especially to the guarding of the purity of faith and morals within the whole patriarchate. The following are a few examples of the use of this power.

Peter (300-311), Bishop of Alexandria, deposed Meletius, who had been convicted of many crimes, as St. Athanasius related.[43] Alexander (312-328), the Bishop of Alexandria immediately before the accession of St. Athanasius, deposed Arius and his followers for their crimes against the true faith, as was declared by the church historian Socrates (ca. 380-ca. 450).[44] And St. Athanasius (328-373), in order to promote the increase of the true faith at Ptolemais, transferred Siderius from a small village to that see because Siderius was a man capable of greater undertakings.[45]

When Theophilus was Bishop of Alexandria (385-412), he sent Synesius (407-415), the Bishop of Ptolemais, on ecclesiastical business to Palaebisca. Among other things, Synesius was to hear the case of Paul, Bishop of Erythrum. Later Synesius made a report concerning these things to Theophilus. This report is contained in *Letter 67*, written around 411 by Synesius to Theophilus.[46] The very existence of the letter testifies to the supervisory power of the Bishop of Alexandria over the entire patriarchate. The opening words of it are eloquent in proclaiming the power of the Patriarch over the other bishops, for its author, Synesius, wrote that it was necessary for him to take as a law whatever was decided upon by the Bishop of Alexandria.[47]

In *Actio IV* of the Council of Chalcedon (451) one reads that the bishops of Egypt refused to sign the letter of Pope Leo which condemned Eutyches. However, they defended themselves from heresy in this connection by stating that their refusal was not due

---

[43] *Apologia contra Arianos,* c. 59—*MPG,* XXV, 355-358; cf. *infra,* p. 51.

[44] *Historia Ecclesiastica,* Lib. I, cap. 6—*MPG,* LXVII, 42; cf. *infra,* p. 51.

[45] Synesius, *Ep. 67* (Theophilo Alexandrino)—*MPG,* LXVI, 1418; cf. *supra,* p. 48.

[46] *Notae Petavii*—*MPG,* LXVI, 1411.

[47] Synesius, *Ep. 67* (Theophilo Alexandrino): "Mihi quidem et libet et divina prope imposita necessitas est pro lege id habendi quidquid thronus ille statuerit."—*MPG,* LXVI, 1411.

to any opposition to the faith, but rather to a custom that had force in Egypt, in virtue of which the Egyptian Bishops could not sign such a letter without the direction of the Bishop of Alexandria.[48]

Although they were opposed, as is clear from the same *Actio* of the Council, the Egyptian Bishops remained firm in their determination not to sign the letter without authorization from the Bishop of Alexandria and in their appeal to ancient custom.[49] They were asking that the matter be allowed to wait until a new Bishop had been ordained for the vacant see of Alexandria, a request that was finally granted.[50]

Kurtscheid recognized as a patriarchal right the prerogative of exercising a general vigilance over the entire patriarchate.[51]

---

[48] "HIERACUS REV EPS AEGYPTI ET CETERI REVV EPI AEGYPTII PER EUNDEM HIERACUM DD: '. . . sanctissimi patres qui in Nicaea congregati sunt trecenti decem et octo regulam dederunt ut sequatur omnis Aegyptiaca regio archiepiscopum magni nominis Alexandrinae ciuitatis et nihil absque ipsum agatur ab aliquo ei subjacente episcopo.' "—Schwartz, *Concilium Universale Chalcedonense,* Vol. III, pars altera, p. 116.

[49] ". . . si extra voluntatem praesidis nostri aliquid faciamus, sicut praesumptores et non seruantes secundum canones antiquam consuetudinem omnes Aegypticae regionis insurgunt in nos. . . ."—*ibid.,* p. 117.

[50] Actio IV: "MAGNIFICENT ET GLORIOSSIMI JUDICES ET AMPLISSIMUS SENATUS DD: Quoniam reuerentissimi episcopi Aegyptiorum non ut repugnantes catholicae fidei suscribere in praesenti distulerunt epistulae sanctissimi archiepiscopi Leonis, sed dicentes consuetudinem esse in Aegyptiaca regione extra sententiam et iussionem archiepiscopi nihil tale facere, poscunt autem sustineri se, donec consecretur episcopus, qui ordinandus est magnae ciuitatis Alexandriae, rationabile nobis et clemens esse apparuit ut in eodem habitu expectent in regia ciuitate et dilationem habeant usque ad ordinationem archiepiscopi magnae ciuitatis Alexandriae.

"PASCASINUS VIR REV EPS VICARIUS SEDIS APOSTOLICAE D: Si praecipit gloria uestra et jubetis illis aliquid praestari humanitatis, fideiussoribus datis non exeant de ista ciuitate, quamdiu Alexandria episcopum accipiat.

"MAGNIFICENT ET GLORIOSISSIMI IVDICES ET AMPLISSIMVS SENATVS DD: Sanctissimi Pascasini Episcopi sit firmum judicium. Unde permanentes in proprio habitu reuerentissimi episcopi Aegyptiorum aut dent fideiussores, si hoc illis est possibile, aut per sacramenta eis credatur quia expectant ordinationem futuri episcopi magnae ciuitatis Alexandriae. . . ."—*ibid.,* pp. 118-119.

[51] "Ius vigilandi ut leges ecclesiasticae in universo territorio sibi commisso serventur, . . ."—Kurtscheid, I, 122.

D) The Rights Pertaining to Patriarchal Synods

The Bishop of Alexandria had the privilege of convening and presiding over synods composed of all the bishops in the territory over which he exercised patriarchal jurisdiction. In this his power was the same as that of the Bishop of Antioch over the patriarchal synods held there, and it was based on the same legal foundations.[52]

St. Athanasius, Bishop of Alexandria (328-373), wrote that Peter (300-311), one of his predecessors in the bishopric, deposed Meletius in a common synod of bishops.[53] And Socrates in his *Historia Ecclesiastica* related that Alexander, the immediate predecessor of Athanasius on the throne of Alexandria, deposed Arius and his followers after a council of many bishops had been gathered together.[54]

Although these texts do not explicitly state that the synods referred to were convoked by the Bishop of Alexandria, they leave no doubt as to the fact that he presided at them. It seems that one must conclude, therefore, that these synods were also convoked by the Bishop of Alexandria, who thus made use of a power which he possessed in virtue of his superior authority over the other bishops of his patriarchal diocese.

Kurtscheid acknowledged that the Bishop of Alexandria enjoyed the right of convoking in synod the Bishops subject to him,[55] and he indicated two synods held at Alexandria, one in 320, the other in 430, as examples of patriarchal synods.[56] Wernz-Vidal stated that through ancient custom the patriarchs had the right of convoking and directing patriarchal councils.[57]

---

[52] The power of the Bishop of Antioch with regard to the convocation of patriarchal synods and his privilege of presiding over them has already been treated. Cf. *supra*, pp. 43-45.

[53] *Apologia contra Arianos*, c. 59: "Petrus apud nos ante persecutionem episcopus . . . Meletium qui episcopus in Aegypto erat, plurimorum convictum scelerum, in communi episcoporum synodo deposuit."—*MPG*, XXV, 355-358.

[54] *Historia Ecclesiastica*, lib. I, cap. 6: ". . . cum audiret ac cerneret Alexander, gravi exarsit ira et, collecto multorum episcoporum concilio, Arium et reliquos qui sententiam ejus amplectebantur, gradu movit, . . ."—*MPG*, LXVII, 42.

[55] Kurtscheid, I, 120 and 122.

[56] *Ibid.*, p. 143.

[57] Wernz-Vidal, II, 652.

E) The Patriarchal Power Relative to Absolution From Excommunication

The absolution from ecclesiastical penalties imposed for great crimes seems to have been reserved to the Patriarch in the patriarchate of Alexandria.

Eusebius of Nicomedia (d. ca. 342), an Arian bishop, recognized that the Bishop of Alexandria enjoyed the power of receiving back into ecclesiastical communion those who had been excommunicated, for he wrote to Alexander, Bishop of Alexandria (312-328), asking him to receive the Arians back into the Church.[58]

The Emperor Constantine (306-337) recognized that the Bishop of Alexandria had the power of receiving heretics upon their reconciliation back into the communion of the Church, for he commanded St. Athanasius, Bishop of Alexandria, to receive the Arians back into the Church, and this under threat of deposition.[59]

Synesius, Bishop of Ptolemais (407-415), related that he was commanded by the Bishop of Alexandria to hear a case in which Jason, a priest, accused Lamponianus, one of his colleagues, of injuring him. Synesius related that Lamponianus confessed the crime, and thereupon suffered the punishment which was excommunication. But even though Lamponianus was sorry and the people interceded for him, Synesius refused to remove the excommunication, since the absolution from it was reserved to the Bishop of Alexandria. Thus he stated in his letter to Theophilus of Alexandria that the absolution was to be sought from him.[60]

---

[58] Socrates, *Historia Ecclesiastica,* Lib. I, cap. 6: "Eusebius vero Nicomediensis, et quotquot opinionem Arii amplectebantur, ad Alexandrum scripserunt, ut latam iam excommunicationis sententiam dissolveret, et excommunicatos ad Ecclesiam revocaret."—*MPG,* LXVII, 54.

[59] *Apologia contra Arianos,* c. 59: ". . . imperatori beatae memoriae Constantino auctor fuit, ut mihi rescriberet, interminatus ni Arianos admitterem ad communionem, me iis affectum iri malis, quibus et iam olim et haud ita pridem sum affectus."—*MPG,* XXV, 355-358.

[60] Synesius, *Ep. LXVII* (Theophilo Alexandrino): "Sed ego in iis perseveravi, quae semel decreveram; solvendi porro jus, et auctoritatem ad pontificiam sedem rejeci. Unum hoc ergo mihi sumpsi, si Lamponiano fatalis necessitas immineret, et praestituta mortis dies adesse videretur; tum omnibus, qui eo tempore adessent, presbyteris concessi, ut eum communioni restituerent. Nemo enim, quantum in me erit, ecclesiasticis vinculis obstrictus

Section 3. The Patriarchate of Rome

The Bishop of Rome, in virtue of his primatial jurisdiction over the entire Church as successor to St. Peter, always was the supreme ecclesiastical authority on earth. In virtue of his patriarchal jurisdiction, however, he exercised a closer supervision over all the regions of the West, somewhat similar to that exercised by the great Eastern Patriarchs over their patriarchal territory. The geographical extent of the Roman patriarchate has already been treated;[61] it remains but to point out, to the extent that the present writer has been able to discover them, the patriarchal rights anciently enjoyed by the Bishops of the Roman See as Patriarchs.

First, however, it must be recalled that the patriarchal rights were not the same in all the patriarchates;[62] neither were the same rights always exercised in an identical way, even though these were enjoyed in common by the different patriarchs. Thus the Popes from the time of Pope Damasus (366-384) until the sixth century exercised their patriarchal rights in Eastern Illyricum at least to some extent through a Vicar; the other patriarchs, to the knowledge of the present writer, did not have permanent Vicars of this kind. From this one can also conclude, as Hefele stated, that "the Bishop of Rome did not exercise his patriarchal right in the same way in all the West."[63]

While keeping these things in mind, one must not overlook the fact that "in the Roman Pontiff the dignity of Patriarch of the West was not always rigorously distinguished from his primacy of jurisdiction."[64] It is true that among the papal enactments and charges some were intended for the entire Roman patriarchate, but these were few. Grisar explained their comparative rarity by stating that "the Popes usually preferred to address themselves to the whole Church whenever a matter was of sufficient importance to concern the whole wide Western Patriarchate."[65]

---

moriatur. Sin convaluerit, rursus iisdem poenis teneatur, atque a divina humanissimaque anima tua indulgentiae tesseram exspectet."—*MPG,* LXVI, 1426-1427.

[61] *Supra,* pp. 13-16.

[62] *Supra,* p. 39.

[63] *Histoire des Conciles,* I, 566.

[64] Wernz-Vidal, II, 641-642; Kurtscheid, I, 124.

[65] *History of Rome,* I, 344.

Kurtscheid listed two ways in which the patriarchal power of the Bishop of Rome was manifested: namely, "in the jurisdiction which he exercised over metropolitans and in the convocation of synods."[66] Hefele wrote that the Bishop of Rome "exercised his patriarchal right in convoking some general and particular Councils of the Church of the West, for example, the Council of Arles in 314, and in judging the metropolitans of the West, whether this was done in a mediate way, as in Illyricum by his vicar, or in an immediate way."[67]

A) Patriarchal Power of the Bishop of Rome Over the Elevation of Bishops

Until about the middle of the fourth century there was only one Church province in Italy, the Roman province; hence there was only one metropolitan in all Italy during that time, the Bishop of Rome.[68] About the year 350, however, Milan had already become the metropolis of another ecclesiastical province. At the beginning of the fifth century, Aquileia became an ecclesiastical metropolitan see after its detachment from Milan; and Ravenna soon followed Aquileia to the rank of a metropolitan see.[69] Kurtscheid expressly stated that Ravenna acquired the rights of a metropolitan see in 431.[70] Another metropolitan see was established at Salona in Western Illyricum, and it seems that one was also established at Caralis (Cagliari on the Island of Sardinia).[71]

Regarding the patriarchal rights of the Bishop of Rome relative to the consecration of these metropolitans, it is necessary to distinguish, for the practice was not uniform. According to Grisar, the Metropolitan of Ravenna was obliged to be consecrated at Rome, but the consecration in turn had to be preceded by an examination of the acts of the election.[72] Kurtscheid declared that the Roman Pontiffs reserved to themselves the confirmation and conse-

---

[66] Kurtscheid, I, 123.

[67] *Histoire des Conciles,* I, 566.

[68] Grisar, *History of Rome,* I, 346; Kurtscheid, I, 118.

[69] Grisar, *History of Rome,* I, 346-347.

[70] Kurtscheid, I, 118.

[71] Grisar, *History of Rome,* I, 346-347.

[72] *Ibid.,* p. 349.

cration of the Metropolitan of Ravenna.[73] At an earlier date the Metropolitan of Caralis may have been obliged to receive his consecration at Rome.[74]

At least from the beginning of the fifth century, personal consecration by the Pope was not required in the case of the Metropolitans of Milan and Aquileia, for around that time the Bishop of Aquileia became a Metropolitan, and the Roman Pontiffs granted permission to the Bishops of Milan and Aquileia, each to consecrate the other.[75] From the middle of the fifth century, however, the Bishops of the province of Milan ordained their own metropolitan after papal confirmation had been given.[76]

Personal consecration by the Pope was not essential in the case of the metropolitan of Salona. Grisar stated that his election had to be ratified at Rome, and that after this he could be consecrated by the Bishops of his own church province.[77]

In Eastern Illyricum the Pope exercised his patriarchal right of consecrating the metropolitans through his Vicar, the Bishop of Thessalonica. Thus Pope Leo I (440-461) in a letter written in 444 to Anastasius, the Bishop of Thessalonica and Vicar Apostolic of Eastern Illyricum, stated that it was his desire that the metropolitans in that district be ordained by Anastasius.[78]

Grisar declared that the early metropolitans of the more remote church provinces of the patriarchate of the West "announced their

---

[73] Kurtscheid, I, 118.

[74] Grisar, *History of Rome,* I, 349.

[75] Pelagius I (556-561), *Ep.* (ad Joanni Patricio caburtario): "Is mos antiquus fuit, ut quia pro longinquitate vel difficultate itineris ab apostolico onerosum illis fuerat ordinari, ipsi se invicem Mediolanensis et Aquileiensis ordinare episcopi debuissent: ita tamen ut in ea civitate in qua erat ordinandus episcopus, alterius civitatis pontifex occurrere debuisset; ut et ordinandi electio a praesenti ordinatore, ex consensu universalis cui praeficiendus erat Ecclesiae, melius ac facilius potuisset agnosci; et in sua qui ad episcopatum provehendus erat, nec tamen ordinatori suo subdendus fuerat, ordinaretur Ecclesia."—*MPL,* LXIX, 411; Kurtscheid, I, 118; Jaffé, n. 983.

[76] Kurtscheid, I, 118.

[77] *History of Rome,* I, 349.

[78] Leo I, *Ep.* VI (ad Anastasium Thessalonicensem Episcopum), cap. IV: ". . . Singulis autem metropolitanis sicut potestas ista committitur, ut in suis provinciis jus habeat ordinandi, ita eos metropolitanos a te volumus ordinari, maturo tamen et decocto judicio."—*MPL,* LIV, 618-619; Jaffé, n. 404.

installation to the Pope only after having been elected and consecrated, and then received in turn, from Peter's successor, the usual brief assuring them of their communion with Rome."[79]

B) Patriarchal Synods

In the West, patriarchal power was manifested in the convocation of some synods by the Bishop of Rome.[80]

It should be noted, however, that, as Grisar reminded his readers, the Bishop of Rome as metropolitan of the Roman province also enjoyed the right of convoking Bishops in council, and that this function "was scarcely distinguished by the Pope from those actions which he performed as Patriarch of the West or as Supreme Pontiff."[81]

In a treatise on patriarchal synods, Kurtscheid stated that from the end of the sixth century synods of this kind were sometimes convoked by the Pope. At these it was his wont to preside, and in attendance were the metropolitans of Milan, Ravenna, and Aquileia.[82] Kurtscheid mentioned two examples of patriarchal synods held in Rome under Pope Gregory the Great, one in 595, and another in 601.[83] And Hefele-Leclercq mentioned an earlier synod, that of Arles (314), as one for whose convocation the patriarchal right of the Bishop of Rome was exercised.[84]

---

[79] *History of Rome,* I, 349.

[80] *Supra,* p. 54.

[81] *History of Rome,* I, 348.

[82] Kurtscheid, I, 143.

[83] *Loc. cit.;* Mansi, IX, 1226: X, 486.

[84] *Supra,* p. 54.

PART TWO

The Patriarchs in the Middle Ages

In this part of the dissertation the writer proposes to give some of the more important historical data and legal enactments concerning patriarchs from the time of Pope Nicholas I (858-867) up to and including the Council of Florence (1439-1445).

The patriarchal rank, as it originated in antiquity, became what it was through the force of custom as induced by long-continued usage. What this custom had established became subsequently confirmed in written law at the Council of Nicaea (325).[1] In the early history of the patriarchal rank one meets indeed with a few direct pronouncements concerning the individual patriarchal rights and duties. But as time passed there were also many papal pronouncements and some imperial decrees concerning the status of the patriarchs.

From these papal pronouncements one learns not only of the nature of the patriarchal office, but also of the papal objection to the attempts of the Bishops of Constantinople to raise their see in dignity and rank over the other major sees of the East.

Imperial enactments were *of themselves* worthless as sources for the existence of patriarchal jurisdiction, for such jurisdiction could originate only from the Church. Nevertheless, it was possible for the Church to ratify imperial enactments subsequently, and thus give them the force of ecclesiastical law.

This second part of the dissertation will be divided into five chapters. The first, which will be chapter III of the dissertation, will deal with the teaching of Pope Nicholas I (858-867) regarding patriarchs in his reply to the questions of the Bulgarians; chapter IV will treat of the legislation of the IV Council of Constantinople (869-870) as it pertained to patriarchs; chapter V will consider the patriarchs of the Latin rite who were set up in the major Eastern sees during the times of the Crusades; chapter VI will explore the enactments of the IV Lateran Council (1215) concerning patriarchs and patriarchal sees; and chapter VII will center on the Council of Florence (1439-1445), held under Pope Eugene IV (1431-1447). In this last chapter special notice will be taken of the order of precedence followed in the seating arrangement of patriarchs at this Council, and of the pronouncement regarding patriarchs as contained in the decree *Laetentur coeli.*

[1] Canon 6. Cf. *supra*, p. 3.

CHAPTER III

The Patriarchs According to Pope Nicholas I (858-867)

The Bulgarians were converted by Greek missionaries in the early middle ages. Prince Boris (843-888), their leader, became a Christian in 864, taking the name of Michael at baptism, since Emperor Michael III (842-867) had himself assumed the rôle of sponsor.[1]

Pope Nicholas, in answer to 106 questions on the teaching and discipline of the Church submitted by Prince Boris, wrote a letter containing his famous *106 responsa ad consulta Bulgarorum* in the year 866. Among these *responsa,* nn. *92* and *93* dealt with the patriarchs.

In *responsum 92,* the Pope explicitly stated that the true patriarchs were the Bishops of Rome, Alexandria, and Antioch.[2] He was not unaware of the claims of Constantinople and Jerusalem, for he mentioned that, although these Bishops were called Patriarchs, they did not derive this status from the same high authority as did the other three.[3] He then indicated the source from which the Bishops of Constantinople obtained their patriarchal title, stating that it derived from imperial favor rather than through any other reason.[4]

---

[1] Funk, *Church History,* I, 261; Kirsch, "Nicholas I, Saint, Pope"—*Catholic Encyclopedia,* XI, 54-55.

[2] *Ep. XCIX,* cap. 92: "Veraciter illi habendi sunt patriarchae, qui sedes apostolicas per successiones pontificum optinent, id est qui illis praesunt ecclesiis, quas apostoli instituisse probantur, Romanam videlicet, Alexandrinam et Antiochenam."—*MGH,* Epistolarum Tom. VI, *Epistolae Karolini Aevi,* IV, 596; Jaffé, n. 2812.

[3] "Constantinopolitanus autem et Hierosolymitanus antistites, licet dicantur patriarchae, non tantae tamen auctoritatis quantae superiores existunt."—*loc. cit.*

[4] ". . . Constantinopolitanam ecclesiam nec apostolorum quisquam instituit nec Nicena Synodus, quae cunctis synodibus celebrior et venerabilior est, ejus mentionem aliquam fecit, sed solum, quia Constantinopolis nova Roma dicta est, favore principum potius quam ratione patriarcha ejus pontifex appellatus est; . . ."—*ibid.,* pp. 596-597.

Concerning Jerusalem, the Pope, although admitting that the Bishop was also called a Patriarch, did not acknowledge anything more to him than what was already acknowledged by canon 7 of the I Council of Nicaea (325); namely, that in accordance with an ancient custom and tradition he should be honored, but that the dignity of the metropolitan see was to remain intact.[5]

In *responsum 93,* Pope Nicholas definitely stated that Alexandria held second place among the patriarchal sees.[6]

From this response of Pope Nicholas one can conclude that, although the Holy See until the year 866 acquiesced in the use of the patriarchal title, it had nevertheless maintained its original attitude against the claims of Constantinople to a place of precedence over Alexandria and Antioch. But what is to be said about the patriarchal jurisdiction as exercised by the Bishops of Constantinople between the fourth and the ninth centuries? Is this exercise of jurisdiction to be considered as based on valid or on invalid grounds?

In his discussion of the attitude of the Popes relative to the status of Constantinople between the I Council of Constantinople (381) and the IV Council of Constantinople (869-870), Cardinal Pitra declared that the Holy See remained firm not only in its rejection of the canons of Constantinople, Chalcedon, Trullo, and others of the same kind,[7] but also in its demands that Antioch and Alexandria be restored to their rightful dignity. And so it granted to Constantinople and Jerusalem the privilege of honor only, and not the privilege of jurisdiction.[8] The Cardinal considered the 92nd

---

[5] "Hierosolymitanus autem praesul, licet et ipse patriarcha dicatur et secundum antiquam consuetudinem ac Nicenam synodum honorandus sit, salva tamen metropoli propria dignitate, . . ."—*ibid.*, p. 597; cf. Concilium Nicaenum I, canon 7—*supra,* p. 19.

[6] "Porro quis patriarcharum secundus sit a Romano, consulitis. Sed juxta quod sancta Romana tenet ecclesia et Niceni canones innuunt et sancti praesules Romanorum defendunt et ipsa ratio docet, Alexandrinus patriarcharum a Romano papa secundus est."—*MGH, loc. cit.*

[7] Undoubtedly Pitra here referred especially to canon 3 of the I Council of Constantinople (381), and canon 28 of the Council of Chalcedon (451).

[8] ". . . Verissimum est sedem apostolicam sibi constantem fuisse semper, tum ut canones constantinopolitanos, chalcedonenses, trullanos, alios id genus, respingeret; tum ut antiochenam, alexandrinamque cathedras suae restitueret

response of Pope Nicholas to the Bulgarians as a kind of solemn pronouncement to this effect.[9]

However, it seems proper to distinguish between jurisdiction explicitly granted and jurisdiction tacitly approved. As far as the present writer could discover, there was no explicit sharing of patriarchal jurisdiction with the Bishops of Constantinople by the Popes prior to the time of Pope Nicholas, as long as one abstracts from canons 9 and 17 of Chalcedon (451). If, therefore, an explicit grant was necessary, it seems that in consequence one would necessarily have to maintain that all the acts of the Bishops of Constantinople which essentially presupposed this patriarchal jurisdiction for their valid exercise were indeed invalid during that period.

It is not established, however, that an explicit grant was necessary. A tacit papal approval of the putative jurisdiction exercised by the Bishops of Constantinople would have sufficed to render valid all those patriarchal acts. Can it be maintained that, by their silence, the Popes gave this tacit approval?

It has already been stated that after the time of Justinian the Popes no longer protested "regarding the position of Constantinople as one of the Eastern patriarchates."[10] Thus for three centuries the Bishops of Constantinople *de facto* exercised powers which in consequence of an explicit grant would have connoted the possession of true patriarchal jurisdiction, and this they did without any further reproach from Rome. During that time these powers were exercised by Bishops, of whom some at least would have abhorred all acts of usurpation, since this would have been inconsistent with the sanctity of their lives. To them, therefore, their exercise of these powers must have appeared as based on the possession of true jurisdiction. And so it seems that one must maintain that the Patriarchs of Constantinople, at some time between the sixth and the ninth centuries, did acquire a true patri-

---

sublimitati; unde non iurisdictionis, sed honoris tantum privilegia Constantinopoli et Hierosolymae concederet. . . ."—Pitra, *Iuris Ecclesiastici Graecorum Historia et Monumenta,* II, xxvii.

[9] ". . . Ita ad Bulgaros Nicolaus, solemni quadam sententia. . . ."—*loc. cit.*

[10] Eidenschink, p. 5; cf. *supra,* pp. 33-34.

archal jurisdiction, not by way of explicit grant, but rather by way of tacit approval from the Bishop of Rome.

Cardinal Pitra's statement is correct in declaring that only honorary privileges were conferred on the Bishops of Constantinople, if one interpret his statement as referring to the absence of any explicit grant apart from that contained in canons 9 and 17 of Chalcedon (451). The present writer believes that this statement must, however, be restricted as implying simply the denial of such an *explicit* grant.

Later on it will be seen that an explicit grant eventually was made in favor of the Bishop of Constantinople. This occurred in the IV Council of Constantinople (869-870).[11]

---

[11] Cf. *infra*, pp. 68-71.

CHAPTER IV

Legislation of the IV Council of Constantinople (869-870) Concerning Patriarchs

In the year 869 the VIII General Council of the Church was convoked at Constantinople. It was the IV General Council in the series of general councils held in that city. It was indeed very fitting that the council be held in Constantinople, for its purpose was to put an end to the Photian schism which was then afflicting the Church. Photius (d. 891/898) had been uncanonically elevated to the see of Constantinople after the Emperor had banished Ignatius, the rightful Bishop of Constantinople. Besides the uncanonical procedure of the intrusion of a bishop in a see that was already filled, other canonical irregularities had occurred. Thus there had been a neglect of the interstices required between orders (Photius had received the orders from the lectorate to the episcopate in six days), and the orders had been received from an excommunicated bishop, Asbestas of Syracuse.

Naturally Pope Nicholas I (858-867) did not recognize Photius as the lawful Bishop of Constantinople. Photius, on his part, took violent measures against the Church of Rome, the culminating point of which was the excommunication which he attempted to inflict on the Pope in 867.

When Basil the Macedonian ascended the imperial throne the scene changed, for this emperor was unfriendly to Photius. He interned him in a monastery, restored Ignatius to his see, and continued in friendly relations with Rome.

Shortly after the reign of Basil (867-886) had begun, the IV Council of Constantinople was held. "On October 5, 869, the Council was opened in the Church of St. Sophia under the presidency of the papal legates."[1]

This Council was of considerable importance as far as the patriarchs were concerned, and that in the main for two reasons. It

[1] Schroeder, *General Councils*, pp. 157-158.

changed the century-old order of precedence among the major sees; and it conferred, in an explicit way, a patriarchal jurisdiction on the Bishop of Constantinople.

The legislation regarding patriarchs which is contained in the canons of this Council will be treated in the present chapter. The matter will be arranged in articles under the following headings: 1) A new order among the patriarchal sees; 2) The decrees relative to the election of patriarchs; 3) Some particular points of patriarchal jurisdiction.

ARTICLE 1. A NEW ORDER AMONG THE PATRIARCHS

In the preceding chapter, reference was made to the status of Constantinople and Jerusalem as patriarchal sees in 866. It was pointed out that in the centuries that followed the I Council of Constantinople (381), they acquired the honor of the patriarchal title. In the IV Council of Constantinople (869-870), however, both Constantinople and Jerusalem were expressly granted some jurisdictional powers over metropolitans. Besides this, the Council, in canon 21, made a change in the order of precedence in the hierarchy by giving Constantinople second place. This canon, therefore, contains the first official ecclesiastical recognition of Constantinople as the second see.[2]

Canon 21 is not an explicit statement of the order of precedence in the hierarchy, but it is looked upon as an implicit approval of Constantinople as the second see.[3] Thus after almost five centuries, the place of honor accorded to the See of Constantinople in an illegal manner by canon 3 of the I Council of Constantinople (381) is implicitly approved by Rome.

Circumstances, however, had changed since the fourth century. The Moslems had overrun the other three great Eastern patri-

---

[2] Canon 21: ". . . definimus neminem prorsus mundi potentium quemquam eorum, qui patriarchalibus sedibus praesunt, inhonorare, aut movere a proprio throno tentare, sed omni reverentia et honore dignos judicare; praecipue quidem sanctissimum papam senioris Romae, deinceps autem Constantinopoleos patriarcham, deinde vero Alexandriae, ac Antiochiae atque Hierosolymorum; . . ."—Pitra, *Iuris Ecclesiastici Graecorum Historia et Monumenta,* II, xliii.

[3] Schroeder, *General Councils,* p. 173.

archates, since then these patriarchates were reduced to mere shadows of their former greatness, and the three Patriarchs of Alexandria, Antioch, and Jerusalem were satisfied to live at Constantinople. And so no one remained in the East to dispute the claims of the Bishop of Constantinople, whom circumstances had actually made the most important ecclesiastic in the East and second only to the Bishop of Rome. In addition, it would have been unwise for the Pope to reject this canon, for such action might have led to a complete break between the East and the West. Therefore, as Schroeder wrote, "it was in the interests of peace and union that Adrian II (867-872) granted implicitly what Leo I (440-461) had explicitly denied to Anatolius."[4]

Cardinal Pitra, in his explanation of canons 9, 17, and 28 of the Council of Chalcedon (451) would seem to demand another interpretation of canon 21 of the IV Council of Constantinople (869-870), for he stated that the Bishop of Constantinople did not legally obtain the second place among the patriarchs until the time of Innocent III (1198-1216).[5] However, as will be pointed out in the chapter dealing with the IV Lateran Council (1215),[6] canon 5 of that Council, before explicitly ranking the major sees, stated that it was thereby renewing the ancient privileges of the patriarchal sees.

ARTICLE 2. THE DECREES OF THE IV COUNCIL OF CONSTANTINOPLE RELATIVE TO THE ELECTION OF PATRIARCHS

In view of the irregularities connected with the attempted election of Photius to the See of Constantinople, it was only natural to expect that the Council would make some pronouncements concerning episcopal and patriarchal elections.

In canon 5, the Council stressed the importance of a right inten-

---

[4] *Loc. cit.*

[5] ". . . Vicit Romanorum pontificum reprobatio ut constantinopolitanus antistes non prius inter patriarchas secundus iure haberetur quin Innocentius III, in concilio lateranensi a. 1215, indulserit tandem ut, constituto in Constantinopoli patriarcha latini ritus, secundum ille locum inter pontifices teneret."—Pitra, *Iuris Ecclesiastici Graecorum Historia et Monumenta,* I, 535.

[6] *Infra,* pp. 85-87.

tion in those who were to be elevated to the dignity of patriarch. It decreed in this canon that no senator or layman, who was recently tonsured in the hope of becoming a patriarch and made a cleric or monk, was to ascend to the patriarchal dignity. The reason given was that a man motivated by an intention of this kind, received the tonsure not because of religion or out of love for God or from a hope of increasing in virtue, but rather from a love of glory and of power. Such a one was to be all the more kept from gaining this exalted rank, if he was pressed forward by the Emperor.[7]

Anyone who, with an upright intention, became a monk or cleric, received all the orders observing the interstices, and was found blameless, was, according to canon 5, possessed of the necessary qualifications for election and admittance to the patriarchal office. The interstices, as mentioned by this canon, were satisfied when the cleric spent one complete year as a lector, two as a subdeacon, three as a deacon, and four as a priest.[8]

In canon 13, the Council decreed that the clerics of the cathedral of Constantinople who had tarried in lower orders were to ascend to higher orders, and if they proved worthy, they merited even greater honors when vacancies occurred either through promotion or death. Outsiders, however, joining themselves to these clerics,

---

[7] Canon 5: "... Prioribus ergo canonibus concordantes, definimus, neminem de senatoria dignitate vel mundana conversatione nuper tonsum, sub (super) intentione vel expectatione pontificatus vel patriarchatus honoris, clericum aut monachum factum, ad hujusmodi scandere gradum, licet singulos ordines divini sacerdotii plurimum temporis fecisse probetur. Neque enim propter religionem vel amorem Dei, aut propter expectationem transeundi viam virtutum, sed ob amorem gloriae ac principatus tonsus hujusmodi reperitur. Magis autem coercemus hujusmodi, si ab Imperatoria dignitate ad hoc compellatur. . . ."—Pitra, *Iuris Ecclesiastici Graecorum Historia et Monumenta,* II, xxxix.

[8] Canon 5: ". . . Si vero qui per nullam suspicionem praedictae concupiscentiae et expectationis, sed propter ipsum bonum humilitatis, quae est circa Christum Jesum, abrenuntians mundo, fiat clericus aut monachus, et omnem gradum ecclesiasticum transigens, per definita nunc tempora irreprehensibilis inventus extiterit et probatus, ita ut in gradu lectoris annum compleat, in subdiaconi vero duos, sitque (sicque?) diaconus tribus, et presbyter quatuor annis, bene placuit huic sanctae et universali synodo eligi hunc et admitti. . . ."—*loc. cit.*

were not to receive the dignities and honors due to those who labored a long time.[9] Schroeder in commenting on this law stated that "the Council in this canon aimed to restore in the Constantinopolitan Church the ancient discipline that dignities are to be conferred on those only who are worthy of them, and to prevent the recurrence of a situation such as it was then dealing with. Hereafter the candidates for the higher ecclesiastical offices, especially for that of patriarch, must be chosen from the clergy attached to the cathedral and not from the ranks of outsiders, much less from the ranks of those who are not clerics at all, as had happened in the case of Photius and others. For in the promotion of one of the latter classes, there lurks not only the danger that the Church will be dishonored, but it means also the denial of honor to those who by their long and faithful service in the Church are entitled to it."[10]

In canon 22, the Council declared that in accordance with earlier conciliar legislation the promotions and consecrations of bishops were not to be effected without an election and decree of a college of bishops, and that no lay prince or authority was to intrude himself in the election or promotion of a patriarch or metropolitan or any bishop.[11] The Council, however, stated that should it happen that any layman be invited by the Church to debate and cooperate, then if he so wishes, he is permitted reverently to submit to those admitting him.[12] However, the same canon anathematized any secu-

---

[9] Canon 13: ". . . decernimus et promulgamus, ut magnae ecclesiae clerici, qui in subjectis ordinibus morati sunt, ad majores gradus ascendant, et si digni claruerint, melioribus perfrui mereantur honoribus, cum aliqui eorum, qui in ipsis sunt, aut per incrementum ad superiora ministeria advocati fuerint, aut per communem naturae terminum dormientes defuerint; sed non ex illis qui foris sunt, aliqui se his innectentes, debitas eis qui multo tempore laboraverunt, dignitates vel honores recipiant; ac per hoc inveniantur ecclesiae clerici nullo modo posse proficere. . . ." *ibid.*, p. xl.

[10] Schroeder, *General Councils*, p. 168.

[11] Canon 22: "Promotiones atque consecrationes episcoporum, concordans prioribus conciliis, electione et decreto episcoporum collegii fieri, sancta haec et universalis synodus definit et statuit, atque jure promulgat, neminem laicorum principum vel potentium semet inserere electioni vel promotioni patriarchae vel metropolitae aut cujuslibet episcopi, . . ."—Pitra, *Iuris Ecclesiastici Graecorum Historia et Monumenta,* II, xliii.

[12] Canon 22: ". . . Si vero quis laicorum ad concertandum et cooperandum ab ecclesia invitatur, licet hujusmodi cum reverentia, si forte voluerit, obtemperare se asciscentibus; taliter enim sibi dignum pastorem regulariter ad ecclesiae suae salutem promoveat."—*loc. cit.*

lar prince or authority or any layman of other dignity who attempted to act against a common, consonant, and canonical ecclesiastical election. And this stigma of anathema was to remain until such time as the offender obeyed and consented to the desire of the Church concerning the election and ordination of its own bishop.[13]

Canon 12 decreed deposition as the punishment to be meted out to any bishop who had received episcopal consecration through the crafty or tyrannical intervention of secular rulers.[14]

ARTICLE 3. SOME PARTICULAR POINTS OF PATRIARCHAL JURISDICTION

In this article there will be considered in separate sections some individual points of patriarchal jurisdiction concerning which one finds legislation in the canons of the IV Council of Constantinople (869-870). In the first section there will be treated the conciliar enactments concerning patriarchal synods; in the second, the legislation relating to judicial powers enjoyed by the patriarchs; and in the third, a conciliar pronouncement dealing with the due subjection of the faithful to their patriarch.

Section 1. The Patriarchal Synod

At the very beginning of canon 17, the IV Council of Constantinople noted that the I Council of Nicaea (325) had ordered that the ancient custom then prevailing in Egypt be retained, thus recognizing that the Bishop of Alexandria, already at that early

---

[13] Canon 22: ". . . Quisquis autem saecularium principum et potentium, vel alterius dignitatis laicus, adversus communem ac consonantem atque canonicam electionem ecclesiastici ordinis agere tentaverit, anathema sit, donec obediat, ac consentiat, quod ecclesia de electione ac ordinatione proprii praesulis se velle monstraverit."—*loc. cit.*

[14] Canon 12: "Apostolicis et synodicis canonibus, promotiones et consecrationes episcoporum, ex potentia et praeceptione principum factas, penitus interdicentibus, concordantes, definimus et sententiam nos quoque proferimus, ut si quis episcopus per versutiam vel tyrannidem principum hujusmodi dignitatis consecrationem susceperit, deponatur omnimodis, utpote qui non ex voluntate Dei, et ritu ac decreto ecclesiastico, sed ex voluntate carnalis sensus ex hominibus et per homines Dei donum possidere voluit vel consensit."—*ibid.*, II, xl.

date, had long enjoyed power over definite provinces in that region. Canon 17 then decreed that this *prisca consuetudo* of Alexandria be conserved in all things in Old Rome, in New Rome, in Antioch, and in Jerusalem.

It has previously been seen that this *consuetudo* connoted the patriarchal rank.[15] In this canon, therefore, the Council confirmed that rank again for the three old patriarchal sees of Rome, Alexandria, and Antioch. But it also mentioned Constantinople and Jerusalem as sees where this *prisca consuetudo* was to be honored *in omnibus*. Thus one finds, in this canon, the first explicit granting of the patriarchal rank as such to the Bishop of Constantinople.

According to the canon, the Bishops of these sees had power over the metropolitans who received from them either episcopal consecration or the pallium. This power included the right of convoking these metropolitans to meet in synod when necessity urged, and also the right of coercing and correcting them when rumor perhaps had accused them of certain crimes.[16]

In the same canon the Council stated that metropolitans were not to absent themselves from patriarchal synods by offering for their excuse the fact that they held provincial synods in their own province twice a year, and therefore could not attend the synods of the patriarch. The Council recognized patriarchal synods as more useful than provincial synods, and ordered that they be held.[17]

---

[15] *Supra*, pp. 3-4.

[16] Canon 17: "Sancta et universalis nicaena prima synodus antiquam consuetudinem jubet servari per Aegyptum et provincias, quae sub ipsa sunt, ita ut horum omnium Alexandrinus episcopus habeat potestatem, dicens: 'Quia et in Romanorum civitate hujusmodi mos praevaluit.' Qua pro causa et haec magna et sancta synodus tam in seniori et nova Roma, quam in sede Antiochiae et Hierosolymorum priscam consuetudinem decernit in omnibus conservari, ita ut earum praesules universorum metropolitanorum, qui ab ipsis promoventur, et sive per manus impositionem, sive per pallii dationem, episcopalis dignitatis firmitatem accipiunt, habeant potestatem, videlicet ad convocandum eos, urgente necessitate, ad synodalem conventum, vel etiam ad coercendum illos et corrigendum, quum fama eos super quibusdam delictis forsitan accusaverit. . . ."—Pitra, *Iuris Ecclesiastici Graecorum Historia et Monumenta*, II, xli-xlii.

[17] Canon 17: ". . . Consueverunt autem metropolitani bis in anno synodos facere, ideoque sicut dicunt, ad patriarchale penitus non posse concurrere caput. Sed sancta haec et universalis synodus, nec concilia, quae a metro-

The Council also threatened punishment to metropolitans who refused to obey the summons of their patriarch.[18]

Section 2. Judicial Powers Enjoyed by the Patriarchs

Canon 26 of the IV Council of Constantinople (869-870) treated, among other things, of the right enjoyed by a bishop who believed that he was unjustly dealt with by his metropolitan; namely, to appeal to the patriarch against the decision of the metropolitan.[19] Schroeder stated that, when an appeal of this kind was made to the patriarch, he was to decide the matter together with the other metropolitans subject to him.[20]

The Council also declared that metropolitans and bishops were not to be judged by the neighboring metropolitans, even though

---

politanis fiunt, interdicens, multo magis illa novit rationabiliora esse ac utiliora metropolitanorum conciliis, quae a partiarchali sede congregantur, et idcirco haec fieri exigit: a metropolita quippe unius quidem provinciae dispositio efficitur, a patriarcha vero saepe totius causa dioeceseos dispensatur. Ac per hoc communis utilitas providetur, propter quod et speciale lucrum propter generale bonum postponi convenit, cum a majoribus super haec facta fuerit advocatio. Quamvis apud quosdam metropolitanorum antiqua consuetudo et canonica traditio per contemptum ipsorum postposita videantur, non currentibus eis ad communem profectum, quos leges ecclesiae severe condemnantes, omni excusatione remota, subiacere vocationibus proprii patriarchae, sive cum communiter sive cum sigillatim factae fuerint, exigunt. . . ."—*loc. cit.*

[18] Canon 17: ". . . Quisquis ergo metropolitanorum proprium patriarcham contemserit, et vocationem ejus, quae sive ad unum solum, sive ad plures, sive ad omnes fit, absque validissima aegrotatione, vel paganorum incursu, non obedierit, et per totos duos menses post notitiam vocationis ad proprium venire patriarcham minime festinaverit, vel si quocumque modo latitare aut non cognoscere nuntium ab illo missum tentaverit, segregetur; si vero intra unum annum eamdem contumaciam et inobedientiam demonstraverit, deponatur omnibus modis, et ab omni sacerdotali operatione decidat, atque a dignitate et honore, qui metropolitanis convenit, propellatur. Is autem qui huic definitioni non obedierit, etiam et anathema sit."—*loc. cit.*

[19] Canon 26: ". . . Similiter etiam episcopos concurrere ad patriarchale caput decernimus, qui a metropolitis suis talia se pertulisse fatentur, ut apud patriarcham metropolitarum, qui sub ipso sunt, justam et sine suspicione sententiam, quod movetur negotium, accipiat. . . ."—*ibid.*, II, xliv.

[20] Schroeder, *General Councils*, p. 175.

they had fallen into some crime, for the judgment was reserved to their own patriarch.[21]

Excommunication was the punishment for anyone not acquiescing in the pronouncement of this canon.[22]

Section 3. Subjection of the Faithful to Their Patriarch

In canon 10 the Council forbade the faithful to separate themselves from their proper patriarch, even though they pretended to know some crime of the patriarch. There had to be first of all a diligent examination of the matter and a sentence passed by a synod, and until that time no lay person, monk, or cleric was to separate himself from the communion of his own patriarch. Neither was the name of the patriarch to be omitted from the divine mysteries or office.[23]

Likewise bishops and priests, though they resided in distant places, were commanded to be united to their own metropolitans; and the metropolitans, in turn, to their patriarch.[24]

---

[21] Canon 26: ". . . Insuper etiam nullo modo quisquis metropolitanorum vel episcoporum a vicinis metropolitis provinciae suae iudicetur, licet quidam incurrisse crimina perhibeatur, sed a solo patriarcha proprio iudicetur, cujus sententiam rationabilem et iudicium iustum ac sine suspicione fore decernimus, eo quod apud eum honorabiliores quique colligantur, ac per hoc ratum et firmum penitus sit, quod ab ipso fuerit iudicatum. . . ."—Pitra, *Iuris Ecclesiastici Graecorum Historia et Monumenta,* II, xliv.

[22] Canon 26: ". . . Si quis autem non acquieverit iis, quae a nobis edita sunt, excommunicatus existat."—*loc. cit.*

[23] Canon 10: ". . . iuste et congruenter et haec sancta et universalis synodus definit et statuit, quod nullus laicorum vel monachorum, aut aliquis ex catalogo clericorum ante diligentem examinationem et synodicam sententiam a communione se separet proprii patriarchae, licet criminalem quamlibet causam ejus se nosse praetendat; sed neque recuset nomen ipsius referre inter divina mysteria vel officia. . . ."—*ibid.,* p. xl.

[24] Canon 10: ". . . Similiter autem episcopos et presbyteros, qui in exterioribus civitatibus et regionibus sunt, erga proprios metropolitas affectare mandamus. Quod etiam circa patriarcham suum facere metropolitas oportet. . . ."—*loc. cit.*

CHAPTER V

Patriarchs of the Latin Rite in the Major Eastern Sees

Under the phrase "Latin Patriarchs" reference is made in this chapter precisely to those Catholic Patriarchs of the Latin rite who became established in the four major Eastern Sees during the times of the Crusades, and to their successors. These Latin Patriarchs will be considered in this chapter in three articles: the first will treat of the origin of the Latin patriarchates in the East; the second will deal with the privileges and powers enjoyed by the Latin patriarchs; and the third will relate briefly to the length of time that these patriarchs actually held the sees in the East, and to the subsequent history of these Latin patriarchates.

Article 1. The Origin of the Latin Patriarchates in the East

The first Crusaders went to the East around the end of the eleventh century. They took Antioch in 1098 on their way to the Holy Land, and then went on to take Jerusalem, which fell into their hands in 1099. It was after the taking of Antioch in 1098 that Latin Patriarchs began to be created for the great Eastern Sees.[1]

When these Crusaders took Antioch, John III (IV) was the Oriental Patriarch of that See. But since the customs and ceremonies of the Latins were not pleasing to him, he left the city within two years and went to Constantinople. Thereupon a Latin Bishop, Bernard of Artasium in the Principality of Antioch, was made Patriarch of Antioch. He administered that see for thirty-six years.[2]

---

[1] "Patriarchae ritus Latini creari coeperunt in Orientis partibus, post expugnatam a Francis et Latinis urbem Antiochiam anno 1098. . . ."—Le Quien, *Oriens Christianus, in Quattuor Patriarchatus digestus* (3 toms., Parisiis, 1740), III, 785 (hereafter cited as Le Quien).

[2] ". . . Huic . . . ecclesiae (Antiochenae) tunc (1098) praeerat Joannes III, Graeci ritus Patriarcha: et quia sibi non arridebant Latinorum mores et ceremoniae, dimisit eam sedem intra biennium, et Constantinopolim successit

Fortescue stated that "as long as the Orthodox patriarch (John IV) remained there they [the Crusaders] tried to make him a Catholic instead of appointing a rival. However, when at last he fled to Constantinople they considered the see vacant, and Bernard, Bishop of Arthesia, a Frenchman, was elected to it."[3]

After the Oriental Patriarch of Jerusalem, Simeon, who had fled to Cyprus out of fear of the Mohammedans in 1099, died there in the same year, a Latin Patriarch was placed over the See of Jerusalem. The first Latin Patriarch of this See was Dagobert, Bishop of Pisa (1099-1107).[4]

Ipsi itaque principes exercitus Cruce signatorum praesulem Latinum suffecerunt."—*loc. cit.;* "Quando Antiochia in Latinorum potestatem venit anno 1098, . . . Patriarcha Graecus sedebat Joannes, qui egregius nominis Christi sub Saracenis fuerat confessor. Hunc perseverare in sua dignitate ultro permiserunt Latini; verum 'vix evoluto biennio, videns ipse quod non satis utiliter praeesset Graecus Latinis,' inquit Willelmus Tyr. lib. 6, cap. 23, 'urbe cedens, Constantinopolim abiit.' Itaque 'post ejus discessum convenientes ejusdem civitatis clerus et populus, Artasiensem episcopum, Bernardum nomine, natione Valentinum' (id est Valentia ortum in Gallia) 'qui in eadem expeditione D. Podiensem episcopum et legatum sequutus fuerat capellanus ejus, sibi praefecerunt Patriarcham.' . . . Antiochenam sedem adiit Bernardus iste anno 1100 medio circiter, quam ex eodem Tyrio, lib. 14, c. 10 administravit 36 annis."—Le Quien, III, 1153.

[3] Fortescue, "Patriarch and Patriarchate"—*Catholic Encyclopedia,* XI, 551.

[4] ". . . Simili modo, Symeone Patriarcha Hierosolymorum, quo tempore urbs sancta ab iisdem Cruce signatis obsidebatur, defuncto in Cypro insula quo se Mohammedanorum metu receperat, Godefridus Bullonius, Hierosolymis expugnatis, rex a principibus exercitus proclamatus, Patriarcham Latinum, ex iis electum qui expeditionis sacrae comites fuerant, illi subrogari curavit." —Le Quien, III, 785-786. "Postquam urbem Hierosolymam expugnavere Latini anno 1099 die 15 Julii, Godefrido Bullonio duce, hunc quidem principes exercitus crucesignatorum in primum regem elegerunt; deinde, accepto ex insula Cypro Simeonis Patriarchae Hierosolymorum Graeci obitu, de successore illi subrogando deliberatum. 'Dilatio (tamen) facta est,' inquit Albertus Aquensis lib. 6, Hist. Hieros, c. 39, 'donec inveniretur aliquis qui ad hoc pontificale officium foret idoneus, et tantum Arnulphum de Rohes, clericum mirae prudentiae et facundiae, cancellarium sanctae ecclesiae Hierosolymitanae, procuratorem sanctarum reliquiarum, et custodem eleemosinarum fidelium, constituerunt. Promoto nunc Arnulpho ad hanc dignitatem sanctae et novae ecclesiae, donec eligeretur Patriarcha,' etc." (Some writers have claimed this Arnulphus as the first Latin Patriarch. Le Quien refers to them here. Then he continues.) ". . . Constat enim, illo ejecto, . . . Daibertum,

The origin of the Latin Patriarchate of Alexandria and the name of the first Latin incumbent of that See were referred to by Le Quien as being very obscure.[5] He stated that it wasn't clear to him when the line of Patriarchs of Alexandria of the Latin rite commenced, or who was the first of this line. In compiling a list of these patriarchs, he named those from the XIV century onward, who were considered by authors as having enjoyed this dignity.[6]

In Egypt, the Crusaders took Damietta, a coastal city, in 1219, but the Saracens recovered it a little later. The same city was taken again in 1249, this time by St. Louis IX of France (1226-1270), and was for a short time administered by a Latin archbishop. But Louis was forced to restore it to the Mohammedans, and the Archbishop became the metropolitan of Tyre, which then was vacant.[7]

According to Le Quien (1661-1733), it was not until 1365 that the Latins took the city of Alexandria for themselves. But they left it immediately, and so no Latin rite bishop occupied the episcopal throne in that city at that time.[8]

---

quem Daimbertum, Dagobertum, et Theodebertum nominatum a diversis legimus, jam Pisanum episcopum, virum doctrina et facundia celebrem, . . . in Patriarcham Hierosolymorum, . . . fuisse electum. . . ."—*ibid.*, pp. 1243-1245.

[5] "Quod ad Patriarchas Latinos Alexandriae attinet, hinc inde quidem hujusmodi Patriarcharum mentio aliqua occurrit apud scriptores: verum quandonam institui coeperit Latinus iste Patriarchatus, quisve primus illorum Patriarcharum fuerit constitutus, obscurissimum est; . . ."—*ibid.*, p. 786. Cf. also pp. 1143, 1144.

[6] ". . . non tamen mihi constat quandonam inceperit illa Patriarcharum Alexandrinorum ritus Latini series, quisnamve fuerit eorum primus. Eos itaque subjiciam, qui a saeculo XIV hac dignitate instructi a scriptoribus perhibentur."—*ibid.*, pp. 1143-1144.

[7] "Damiatam quidem maritimam Aegypti urbem anno 1219 die 5 Novembris, sibi Cruce signati subjecerunt, sed eamdem paulopost recuperarunt Saraceni. Hanc rursum a S. Ludovico Francorum rege anno 1249 praefatis infidelibus ereptam, brevi admodum sub archiepiscopi titulo praesul administravit Latinus, eam enim Mohammedanis restituere coactus est Ludovicus; praesul vero ad Tyri metropolim tunc vacantem transiit."—Le Quien, III, 786.

[8] ". . . non . . . Latini principes Alexandria urbe potiti sunt, nisi anno 1365, quo eam Petrus rex Cypri coepit, et statim reliquit, ita ut nullus antistes ritus Latini in ea urbe reipsa unquam sederit. . . ."—*loc. cit.*

In the early years of the thirteenth century, the Melchite Patriarch of Alexandria was Nicholas I. This Patriarch was friendly towards Rome, wrote to Pope Innocent III (1198-1216) and to Pope Honorius III (1216-1227), and was invited to be present at the IV Lateran Council in 1215. There seems to have been a special reason, therefore, why a Latin patriarch should not have been set up in his place at that time.[9] However, in the article "Alexandria" in the *Catholic Encyclopedia,* it is stated that "the establishment of the Latin patriarchate [of Alexandria] occurred in 1215. This is clear from the Twelfth General Council (Fourth Lateran), held in that year." There it is also declared that a Latin patriarch was actually appointed for Alexandria in the pontificate of Innocent III, although the author stated that the date was uncertain, as was also the identity of the first patriarch.[10]

Le Quien, on the other hand, assigned first place among the Latin Patriarchs of Alexandria to a certain Aegidius, who had been previously the Patriarch of Grado, and who was made Patriarch of Alexandria by Pope Clement V in 1310. In making this choice the author stated that he could not discover anyone prior to Aegidius in this office.[11]

---

[9] ". . . Saeculo autem decimo-tertio ineunte hujus ecclesiae Melchitis Nicolaus praesidebat, qui Innocentii III Papae fovebat communionem, ut ex epistolis constat quas sibi mutuo scripserunt. Raynald. ad annum 1223 num. 9 refert ejus epistolam ad Honorium III cujus titulus est: *'Reverendo Patri ac Domino Honorio Dei gratia sanctae Romanae ecclesiae summo Pontifici, et universali Papae, Nicolaus eadem gratia Alexandrinae sedis humilis Patriarcha, tam promptam quam debitam reverentiam.'* "—*loc. cit.*; ". . . Verum eo anno (1215) sedebat Patriarcha Alexandrinus Graecus Melchita Nicolaus, cui profecto, utpote ecclesiae Romanae addicto . . . alium Patriarcham Romani Pontifices non substituerunt. . . ."—*ibid.*, p. 1143; Hefele, referring to the attendance of the Patriarchs at the IV Lateran Council (1215) stated that the Melchite Patriarch of Alexandria sent a deacon to attend: "Le patriarche d'Alexandrie (Melchite), soumis à la domination musulmane, n' avait pu envoyer qu' un diacre."—Hefele-Leclercq, *Histoire des Conciles,* V, 1318.

[10] Woods, "Alexandria, The Church of."—*Catholic Encyclopedia,* I, 302.

[11] "Quod spectat ad Aegidium (quem ideo primum assigno Patriarcham Alexandrinum ritus Latini, quia me fugit quis fuerit alius eo antiquior in illa dignitate,) Ughellus in Patriarchis Gradensibus, tom. 5, Italiae Sacrae col. 1214 vet. edit. num 48 D haec de eo habet: 'Frater Aegidius, Ferrariensis,

Fortescue, in his article "Patriarch and Patriarchate" in the *Catholic Encyclopedia,* agreed with Le Quien concerning the first Latin patriarch of Alexandria, for he wrote:

> In 1167 Amaury II, King of Jerusalem, captured Alexandria, as did Peter I, King of Cyprus, in 1365. But both times the city was given back to the Moslems at once. Nor were there any Latin inhabitants to justify the establishment of a Latin patriarchate. On the other hand, the Orthodox patriarch, Nicholas I (c. 1210- after 1223; Le Quien II, 490) was well disposed towards reunion, wrote friendly letters to the pope, and was invited to the Fourth Lateran Council (1215). There was then a special reason for not setting up a Latin rival to him. Eventually a Latin patriarchate was established rather to complete what had been done in other cases than for any practical reason. Giles, Patriarch of Grado, a Dominican, was made first Latin Patriarch of Alexandria by Clement V in 1310. An earlier Latin Athanasius seems to be mythical (Le Quien, III, 1143).[12]

Whoever the first Latin patriarch of Alexandria may have been, or whatever the time of his appointment, it is indicated in the *Annuario Pontificio* that the patriarchs of this line were never residential patriarchs, but merely titulars.[13]

Constantinople also received a Latin patriarch, but not until the thirteenth century at the time of the fourth Crusade.[14] When the Crusaders captured the city, the Greek Patriarch fled, and the conquerors elected the first Latin Patriarch of Constantinople in 1204.

Ordinis Praed. insignis alumnus, ad sedem Gradensem assumptus est a Bonafacio VIII anno 1295-. . . . Is anno 1308 a Clemente V Papa, una cum FF. Lupo Ord. Praedic. et Athanasio Ord. Min. legatus missus est ad regem Rasciae Vrosium, de quo legendus Odericus Raynaldus to. 15. Translatus deinde est Aegidius a Clemente V ad Alexandrinum Patriarchatum anno 1310 ut in Reg. Vatic. habetur. . . ."—Le Quien, III, 1143.

[12] *Catholic Encyclopedia,* XI, 551.

[13] "Durante le Crociate furono costituiti Patriarcati latini residenziali (meno quello di Alessandria, che fu sempre semplice titolo)."—*Annuario Pontificio* (Città del Vaticano: 1947), p. 83.

[14] ". . . quum inito saeculi XIII urbs Constantinopolitana in potestatem devenisset Cruce signatorum qui in Palaestinam pergebant, illi quoque in ea urbe Latinum sibi praefecerunt Patriarcham."—Le Quien, III, 786.

Thomas Morosini, a Venetian, was the newly elected Patriarch. At first Pope Innocent III declared this election invalid, as having been carried out by clerics not having the power, and by laymen. But later the same Pope, on his own authority, influenced by the petition of the Emperor and also by other just causes, made Thomas the Patriarch, and personally consecrated him during the following year, 1205.[15]

ARTICLE 2. THE AUTHORITY OF THE LATIN PATRIARCHS

In this article the writer proposes to treat of the jurisdiction and the privileges enjoyed by these Latin Patriarchs over their dioceses in the middle ages, that is, during the time they held actual residence there for the government of these sees.

In the first place it must be pointed out that the patriarchal territory over which the Latin patriarchs exercised jurisdiction was not necessarily coextensive with that over which the corresponding Greek patriarchs had formerly presided. Thus Tyre, the metropolitan see of Phoenicia Prima, belonged to the Patriarchate of Antioch from ancient times. But when it was taken by the Latins, it was subjected to the see of Jerusalem. Pope Innocent III (1198-1216) gave his assent to this change, but demanded that the three episcopal sees of Byblus, Antaradus, and Tripolis Syriae be removed from subjection to the metropolitan of Tyre, and remain in the Patriarchate of Antioch.[16] When the Crusaders took Constantinople, however, in 1204, and the Latin patriarchate was erected there, the Churches of the regions then controlled by the Crusaders were assigned to its jurisdiction. But

---

[15] "Superstite licet adhuc Patriarcha Constantinopolitano Graeco Joanne Camatero, qui capta urbe a Francis et Venetis, una cum Niceta, aliisque plurimis, inde recessit, electus est anno 1204 primus ejusdem urbis Patriarcha ritus Latini, Thomas Maurocenus sive Moresini, nobilis Venetus, . . . Hanc tamen electionem Innocentius III nullam primo congressu declaravit, utpote contra canones a clericis ad id potestatem non habentibus, et a laicis factam: Thomam nihilominus sibi optime notum, precibus Balduini Imperat. motus, justasque alias ob causas, sua authoritate renuntiavit Patriarcham, ac suis manibus consecravit anno sequenti 1205."—Le Quien, III, 796-797.

[16] Le Quien, III, 787-788.

Pope Innocent III excluded those Churches which had not formerly been subject to the see of Constantinople.[17]

The special prerogative of the Patriarchs of the Latin rite in the major sees of the East was that of consecrating the metropolitans and archbishops of their patriarchate and of giving them the pallium.[18]

In the Latin patriarchates the chapters of the Churches elected the bishops and metropolitans *de prisco iure.* Bishops thus elected were confirmed and consecrated by their metropolitan, while metropolitans thus elected were confirmed and consecrated by their patriarch.[19]

Le Quien stated that after Palestine and all of Syria had again been taken by the Mohammedans and the Westerners expelled, the canons of the Churches of Antioch and Jerusalem betook themselves elsewhere, apparently to the Island of Cyprus, where in their customary manner they elected successors for the Patriarchs who had recently died.[20] But Pope Boniface VIII (1294-1303) wished to guard against the possibility that some men be named patriarchs without being possessed of the proper qualifications.[21]

[17] "Subsequentem vero petitionem, . . . qua ecclesias illas tibi subjici postulabas, quae priusquam Constantinopolitana civitas caperetur Constantinopolitano Patriarchae minime respondebant, duplici ratione non duximus admittendam, . . ."—Le Quien, III, 788.

[18] "Praecipuam Patriarcharum Latini ritus praerogativam in eo constitisse liquet ex dictis, quod suarum dioecesium metropolitanos et archiepiscopos, tum ordinarent, tum pallio donarent, accepto ab illis prius sacramento, quo sancte sponderent, non Patriarchae duntaxat suo, sed Romanae imprimis sedi obedientes futuros, quemadmodum apud nos fit. . . ."—Le Quien, III, 791.

[19] ". . . Episcoporum itaque et metropolitanorum electio ad ecclesiarum capitula de prisco jure spectabat, episcoporum autem confirmatio et consecratio ad metropolitanos, sicut metropolitanorum ad Patriarcham. Atque haec consuetudo duravit pro uno quoque Patriarchatu, quandiu Patriarchae singuli suarum regionum ecclesias reliquiasve tenuerunt."—*loc. cit.*

[20] "Post Palaestinam omnemque Syriam Mohammedanorum armis iterum subactas, Francis ac Latinis inde ejectis, Antiochenae atque Hierosolymitanae ecclesiarum canonici Latini ritus alio se receperunt, atque, ut apparet, in insulam Cyprum, ibique Patriarcharum ejusdem ritus qui nuper occubuerant successores more pristino elegerunt. . . ."—*loc. cit.*

[21] ". . . At Bonifacius VIII . . . anno 1301 . . . cavendum ducens ne aliqui in Patriarchas renunciarentur qui ad id muneris minus essent idonei, unde Patriarchae nomen et dignitas summa vilesceret, . . ."—*loc. cit.*

Therefore he decreed in 1301 that, as long as the cities of Constantinople, Alexandria, Antioch, and Jerusalem were under the domination of infidels or schismatics, the canons of these patriarchal sees were not to proceed in any way, *sede patriachali vacante,* to the choosing of the next incumbent without the permission of the Holy See.[22]

The return of some Greek schismatic bishops to union with Rome raised a practical difficulty for the Latin Patriarch of Constantinople, since these bishops refused to be anointed with chrism, a ceremony that was customary in episcopal ordinations in the Latin rite. The Patriarch, therefore, asked the Holy See what should be done about it.[23] Pope Innocent III, in his reply given in 1208, distinguished between those Greeks who had already been consecrated Bishops and those who were yet to be consecrated. If the former could not be induced to receive the unction, the Patriarch could pass it by through dissimulation; the latter, however, were not to be consecrated unless they were willing to receive consecration according to the Latin ceremonial, *more latino.*[24]

In 1198, the first year of his pontificate, Pope Innocent III forbade the Latin patriarchs to transfer the bishops of their patri-

---

[22] "Statuit, ut, quamdiu Constantinopolitana, Alexandrina, Antiochena et Ierosolymitana civitates schismaticorum aut infidelium subsunt aut suberunt ditioni, canonici harum patriarchalium sedium, cum eas vacare contigerit, ad electionem, postulationem aut provisionem de praeficiendo sibi patriarcha nullo modo procedant absque apostolicae sedis licentia."—Potthast, *Regesta Pontificum Romanorum inde ab a. post Christum natum MCXCVIII ad a. MCCCIV* (2 vols., Berolini: 1874-1875), n. 25115 (hereafter this work will be cited as Potthast).

[23] Innocentius III, *Regestorum sive Epistolarum Lib. XI, Ep. 23* (Patriarchae Constantinopolitano): "Ex parte tua fuit propositum coram nobis quod quidem Episcopi Graeci ad tuam obedientiam redeuntes, fidelitatis praestiterunt tibi corporaliter juramentum nobisque obedientiam promiserunt, sed inungi renuunt juxta consuetudinem Latinorum. Unde quid super iis agere debeas postulasti per sedem apostolicam edoceri. . . ."—*MPL,* CCXV, 1353.

[24] ". . . Nos igitur inquisitioni tuae taliter respondemus, quod si ii qui jam consecrati sunt induci nequeunt ut recipiant unctionem, id in hac novitate sub dissimulatione poteris pertransire. Consecrandos vero nullatenus consecres, nisi more Latino voluerint consecrari, cum nos ipsi Graecos nonnisi juxta nostram consuetudinem consecremus."—*loc. cit.*

archate from one see to another. This prohibition was contained in a letter written by the Pope to the Latin Patriarch of Antioch.[25]

Privileges and jurisdictional powers enjoyed by the Patriarch Thomas, the first Latin Patriarch of Constantinople, were listed in a letter which Pope Innocent III (1198-1216) wrote to that Patriarch in 1205.

In this letter the Pope declared that all the possessions then rightly belonging to the Church of Constantinople, or which would rightly come into its possession in the future by reason of grants either from ecclesiastical or secular persons, were to remain under the administration of Thomas and his successors.[26] He ratified the liberties and immunities of the Church of Constantinople as well as its ancient and reasonable customs, provided that they were not opposed to the institutes of the Holy See, and sanctioned that these should continue to exist undiminished in the future.[27]

The Pope, besides giving the pallium to the new Patriarch, also gave a detailed explanation of its rightful use. It was to be used only in those Churches which were subject to the jurisdiction of Thomas, that is, during Mass on certain specified occasions.[28] The

---

[25] Innocentius III, *Regestorum sive Epistolarum Lib. I, Ep. 50* (Antiocheno Patriarchae) : "Cum ex illo generali privilegio, quod beato Petro et per eum Ecclesiae Romanae Dominus noster indulsit, canonica postmodum manaverint instituta continentia majores Ecclesiae causas esse ad sedem apostolicam perferendas; ac per hoc translationes episcoporum sicut depositiones eorum et sedium mutationes ad summum apostolicae sedis antistitem de jure pertineant, nec super his praeter ejus assensum aliquid debeat attentari, miramur non modicum et movemur quod tu, . . ."—*MPL,* CCXIV, 45.

[26] Innocentius III, *Regestorum sive Epistolarum Lib. VIII, Ep. 19* (Thomae, Patriarchae Constantinopolitano) : "Praeterea quascumque possessiones, quaecunque bona eadem Ecclesia in praesentiarum juste et canonice possidet, aut in futurum, concessione Pontificum, et ecclesiasticarum seu etiam saecularium personarum, cujuscumque status aut conditionis, . . . poterit adipisci, firma tibi et tuis successoribus illibata permaneant. . . ."—*MPL,* CCXV, 575.

[27] ". . . Libertates quoque et immunitates ejusdem ecclesiae ac consuetudines rationabiles et antiquas, quae apostolicae sedis non obviant institutis, ratas habemus, et eas perpetuis temporibus illibatas permanere sancimus. . . ."—*loc. cit.*

[28] ". . . Palleum quoque, insigne videlicet plenitudinis pontificalis officii, fraternitati tuae, de apostolicae sedis libertate largimur, quo, intra ecclesias

Patriarch was in turn allowed to grant the use of the pallium to the archbishops who were subject to him.[29] Permission was also granted to the Patriarch to have the cross carried before him in any place he chanced to pass through, except in Rome and in any place where the Pope was present.[30]

Before concluding his letter, the Pope decreed that every cleric who obtained a church or ecclesiastical benefice in the Patriarchate of Constantinople, no matter what his race or nation, was to show to the Patriarch and to the Church of Constantinople the proper honor and reverence, with due allowance made for the authority, reverence, and honor of the Holy See.[31]

This letter, replete with papal grants, was sent to the Latin Patriarch of Constantinople in 1205 by Pope Innocent III (1198-1216). However, according to the testimony of Le Quien, it contained a very clear exposition of the form of administration of all

---

tuae jurisdictioni subjectas, in solemniis missarum utaris, diebus inferius denotatis, videlicet in Nativitate Domini, festivitate protomartyris Stephani, Circumcisione Domini, Epiphania, Ypopanti, Dominica in Ramis palmarum, Coena Domini, Sabbato Sancto, Pascha, feria secunda post Pascha, Ascensione, Pentecoste, tribus festivitatibus beatae Mariae, Natalis Joannis Baptistae, solemnitatibus omnium apostolorum, commemoratione sanctorum omnium, dedicationibus ecclesiarum, episcoporum consecrationibus, ordinationibus clericorum, principalibus festivitatibus ecclesiarum tuarum, et anniversario consecrationis tuae die, et tam imperatoris, quam aliorum magnatum et principum sepulturis. . . ."—*loc. cit.* "The Latin Patriarchs were bound to seek the use of the pallium from the Pope and to actually receive it from him."—Le Quien, III, 790.

[29] Innocentius III, *Regestorum sive Epistolarum Lib. VII, Ep. 19* (Thomas, Patriarchae Constantinopolitano): ". . . Ad indicium etiam gratiae plenioris, auctoritate tibi praesentium indulgemus, ut archiepiscopis, suffraganeis tuis, usum pallii praesentis indulgentiae auctoritate concedas, ab eis pro te quod canonicum fuerit, pro nobis autem et Ecclesia Romana sponsionem obedientiae, recepturus. . . ." *MPL,* CCXV, 575.

[30] ". . . Porro crucem, videlicet vexillum Dominicum, per quemcumque locum te transire contigerit, excepta urbe Romana, et loco in quo fuerit Romanus antistes, ante te deferendi, fraternitate tuae licentiam impartimur, . . ." —*loc. cit.*

[31] ". . . Praesenti scripto nihilominus statuentes, ut universi clerici, cujuscumque nationis et gentis, in civitate et dioecesi Constantinopolitana ecclesias vel ecclesiastica beneficia obtinentes tibi et Ecclesiae Constantinopolitanae reverentiam debitam et honorem devotum exhibeant, salva in omnibus auctoritate sedis apostolicae reverentia, et honore. . . ."—*ibid.,* pp. 575-576.

the Latin Patriarchs, whose jurisdictional power was much less than that of the Oriental Patriarchs who presided over the major sees of the East in former times.[82] In quoting Le Quien on this point, one must again call to the attention of the reader the fact that the Latin Patriarchs of Alexandria were never more than mere titular patriarchs.[83]

In another letter to the Latin Patriarch of Constantinople, Pope Innocent III granted still further privileges.[84] Thus he gave Thomas the power of absolving those of his subjects who had laid violent hands on clerics or other religious men. This absolution the Patriarch was to grant with the authority and in the place of the Pope. However, it was to be denied and the delinquent referred to Rome when the enormity of the crime indicated such a procedure.[85]

Another privilege enjoyed by the first Latin Patriarch of Constantinople was that of absolving those who had been guilty of the *vitium falsitatis* against the seal of the Patriarch himself or that of his subjects.[86]

---

[82] "Quum summa esset Patriarcharum Graecorum in omnes dioecesium suarum sedes auctoritas, et praesertim praesulis Constantinopolitani, quae ab ea non discrepabat, qua Romani Pontifices per omnes occiduarum gentium regiones jus dicebant: Patriarcharum Latinorum jurisdictio ad angustiores longe terminos coarctata fuit. Hujus administrationis formam disertissime exponit Innocentius III litteris suis apostolicis, quibus praefati Thomae in primum Patriarcham Constantinopolitanum Latini ritus electionem confirmavit, . . . Recepto enim ab eo fidelitatis et obedientiae juramento, sub tenore antiquo et approbato, quo primates et metropolitani pallium suscipientes uti solent, privilegium Patriarchale his verbis ei concessit. . . ."—Le Quien, III, 789.

[83] *Supra*, p. 76.

[84] Innocentius III, *Regestorum sive Epistolarum Lib. VIII, Ep. 20* (Eidem Thomae, Patriarchae Constantinopolitano): ". . . specialem tibi gratiam facere volumus, et te personaliter intendimus honorare. Eapropter, venerabilis in Christo frater, tuis justis petitionibus annuentes, auctoritate tibi praesentium indulgemus. . . ."—*MPL*, CCXV, 576.

[85] ". . . indulgemus, . . . ut subditos tuos qui in clericos et alios viros religiosos manus injecerint violentas, auctoritate et vice nostra secundum Ecclesiae formam absolvas, nisi forsitan ita fuerit enormis excessus, ut merito credas eos ad sedem apostolicam destinandos: . . ."—*loc. cit.*

[86] ". . . falsariorum quoque absolutionem tuae fraternitati committimus, si forsan in sigillo tuo vel subditorum tuorum vitium commiserint falsitatis. . . ."—*loc. cit.*

And Thomas was also given the privilege of anointing kings if such were to be anointed in the Constantinopolitan Empire, provided that he had been requested to perform the anointing, and that the Emperor had given his consent.[37]

ARTICLE 3. SUBSEQUENT HISTORY OF THE LATIN PATRIARCHS

It was as a result of the Crusades that the Latin Patriarchs became established in the East. The Oriental patriarchal lines did not as a consequence of this come to an end, although the patriarchs, in most cases, did not reside in their sees. There were, consequently, Greek (Melchite) patriarchs and Latin patriarchs for each of the four major sees of the East. These two patriarchal lines have continued ever since.

Fortescue summed up the history of the Latin Patriarchs during the following centuries by stating that ". . . the Latin Patriarchs ruled as long as the Latins held those lands. When the crusaders' kingdoms came to an end they went on as titular patriarchs and have been for many centuries dignitaries of the papal court. . . ."[38]

The Latin Patriarch of Jerusalem, however, has been sent back to Jerusalem and given jurisdiction. His return was decreed by Pope Pius IX (1846-1878), who also restored jurisdiction to the Patriarch with the Apostolic Letter *"Nulla celebrior"* of July 23, 1847.[39]

---

[37] ". . . tibi personaliter indulgemus, ut, si reges in Constantinopolitano imperio fuerint inungendi, dum tamen a te inunctio postuletur, et assensus imperialis accedat, inungas."—*loc. cit.*

[38] "Patriarch and Patriarchate,"—*Catholic Encyclopedia,* XI, 551.

[39] Pius IX, litt. ap. *Nulla celebrior,* 23 iul., 1847: ". . . auctoritate Omnipotentis Dei, et SS. Apostolorum Petri et Pauli, ac Nostra restituimus Hierosolymis exercitium jurisdictionis Latini Patriarchae, eumdem posthac residendi obligationi, ut olim, obnoxium fore declaramus. . . ."—*Acta Pii IX* (9 vols., Romae: 1854-1878), Pars prima, Acta exhibens quae ad Ecclesiam Universam spectant, Vol. I, pp. 59 ff.

CHAPTER VI

THE ENACTMENTS OF THE IV LATERAN COUNCIL (1215) CONCERNING PATRIARCHS AND PATRIARCHAL SEES

In 1215, the IV Lateran Council was convoked by Pope Innocent III (1198-1216). This Council is referred to in canon law as the "Great Council" or the "Great Lateran Council" because of the importance and relatively "large number of its enactments as well as from the number and rank of many who took part in it."[1]

In the history of this council as given in Mansi, there appears a quotation taken from a writing of the Premonstratensian Abbot of Ursberg, who was in attendance at the Council. In this quotation one reads that the Patriarchs of Constantinople and Jerusalem personally attended, and that the Patriarchs of Alexandria and Antioch sent legates.[2] Hefele stated that this Patriarch of Constantinople was the Latin Patriarch Gervais. The Patriarch of Antioch referred to was likewise a Latin Patriarch; the Patriarch of Alexandria, however, was a Melchite.[3]

There were two main issues which prompted the Holy Father

---

[1] Schroeder, *General Councils,* p. 236.

[2] "Cogitur itaque Romae in Lateranensi ecclesia satis magnum concilium: de quo abbas Urspergensis, qui eo tempore floruit, haec habet: 'Anno . . . 1215 . . . celebrata est universalis synodus Romae. . . . In qua fuerunt episcopi 412. Inter quos extiterunt de praecipuis patriarchis duo, videlicet Constantinopolitanus, et Hierosolymitanus: Antiochenus autem gravi languore detentus, venire non potuit; sed misit pro se vicarium Antheradensem episcopum. Alexandrinus vero, sub Saracenorum dominio constitutus fecit quod potuit, mittens pro se diaconum suum Germanum' . . ."—Mansi, XXII, 955. The abbey of Ursberg, in the diocese of Augsburg, had been founded by St. Norbert (d. 1134) under the auspices of Count Werner of Schwabeck, perhaps as early as 1126.—Heimbucher, *Die Orden und Kongregationen der Katholischen Kirche* (3. ed., 2 vols., Paderborn: Schöningh, 1933-1934), I, 437.

[3] *Histoire des Conciles,* V, 1318.

to convoke this council. These were the gaining back of the Holy Land and the reform of the universal Church.[4]

Among the decrees of this Council, canon 5 treated of the patriarchal sees. It confirmed the order and rank among them, and made specific mention of three of their rights. Canon 30 contained mention of another patriarchal right; namely, that of removing the particular suspension inflicted upon bishops who had been contumaciously neglectful about appointing worthy incumbents in ecclesiastical benefices. In the present chapter the enactment of the Council concerning the order and rank of patriarchal precedence will be treated in the first article; the three specific rights mentioned in canon 5 as well as the one stated in canon 30 will be discussed in the second article.

ARTICLE 1. THE ORDER AMONG THE PATRIARCHAL SEES IS CONFIRMED

In canon 5 of the IV Lateran Council (1215) one finds the first explicit statement of a new order among the patriarchal sees. In this law it was clearly stated that Constantinople was the first See after Rome; then Alexandria, Antioch, and Jerusalem were listed in that order.[5]

From the time of the approval of this canon, therefore, since it contained a very clear statement, there can be no question of the order of precedence among the five major sees. On the other hand,

---

[4] ". . . inter omnia desiderabilia cordis nostri duo in hoc saeculo principaliter affectamus: ut ad recuperationem videlicet terrae sanctae, ac reformationem universalis ecclesiae valeamus intendere cum effectu . . . hoc tandem ad exequendum praedicta . . . providimus faciendum, ut quia haec universorum fidelium communem statum respiciunt, generale concilium juxta priscam sanctorum patrum consuetudinem convocemus, propter lucra solummodo animarum opportuno tempore celebrandum: . . ."—Mansi, XXII, 960-961.

[5] Canon 5: "Antiqua patriarchalium sedium privilegia renovantes, sancta universali synodo approbante sancimus, ut post Romanam ecclesiam, quae disponente Domino super omnes alias ordinariae potestatis obtinet principatum, utpote mater universorum Christi fidelium et magistra, Constantinopolitana primum, Alexandrina secundum, Antiochena tertium, Hierosolymitana quartum locum obtineant, . . ."—c. 23, X, *de privilegiis et excessibus privilegiatorum,* V, 33; Mansi, XXII, 989-992.

one cannot agree with the opinion of those who state that this new order was instituted at this time, for the very first words of the canon stated that the ancient privileges of the patriarchal sees were being renewed, *antiqua patriarchalium sedium privilegia renovantes, . . . sancimus . . .* , and these words apply at least to the following clause wherein the order among the five sees is explicitly stated.

The canon, therefore, in stating this order of precedence did not establish new privileges, but simply restated already existing ones. This opinion is held by Schroeder, who in a summary prefixed to canon 5 of the IV Lateran Council stated: "The Council approves the existing order of the patriarchal sees. . . ."[6] But in spite of the fact that this order among the patriarchal sees was not new in 1215, but had been implicitly introduced almost four centuries before with the papal approval of canon 21 of the IV Council of Constantinople (869-870),[7] it was only after the approval of canon 5 of the IV Lateran Council that the Latin Patriarch of Constantinople was formally allowed to take second place.[8]

In defending the opinion that the IV Lateran Council in canon 5 granted merely an explicit recognition to an order of precedence among patriarchs that had already been implicitly established, one must disagree with Cardinal Pitra who stated that the Bishop of Constantinople was not considered legally as second among the patriarchs until Pope Innocent III in 1215 allowed him to take that place.[9] It is difficult to see how the opinion of Pitra can be sustained in view of the opening words of canon 5 of the Lateran

---

[6] Schroeder, *General Councils,* p. 246.

[7] Cf. *supra,* pp. 64-65.

[8] "Though at the Fourth General Council of Constantinople the Roman legates signed the twenty-first canon, which accorded recognition to that city as second in patriarchal rank, it was not till this fifth canon was approved by the council that the Latin patriarch of that see was formally allowed this place."—Schroeder, *General Councils,* p. 246, footnote 10; cf. Hefele-Leclercq, *Histoire des Conciles,* V, 1318.

[9] ". . . constantinopolitanus antistes non prius inter patriarchas secundus iure haberetur quin Innocentius III, in concilio lateranensi a. 1215, indulserit tandem ut, constituto in Constantinopoli patriarcha latini ritus, secundum locum inter pontifices teneret."—Pitra, *Iuris Ecclesiastici Graecorum Historia et Monumenta,* I, 535; cf. *supra,* p. 65.

Council, which stated that ancient patriarchal privileges were being renewed. *"Antiqua patriarchalium sedium privilegia renovantes. . . ."*[10]

ARTICLE 2. OTHER PATRIARCHAL RIGHTS SPECIFICALLY STATED BY THE IV LATERAN COUNCIL

In canon 5 of the IV Lateran Council three other rights of patriarchs were mentioned in addition to their order of precedence. These rights were that of conferring the pallium on their suffragans under certain conditions, that of having the cross carried before them in certain places and circumstances, and that of receiving appeals from provinces subject to their jurisdiction.

The privilege of conferring the pallium was not to be exercised by the patriarchs of the four Eastern sees until such time as they had received the pallium from the Roman Pontiff and had taken an oath of fidelity and obedience to him. After this they could confer the pallium on their own suffragans, receiving for themselves the canonical profession of faith, and for the Roman Church the pledge of obedience from these suffragans.[11]

The privilege of having the cross carried before them could be enjoyed by the patriarchs anywhere except in the city of Rome, or in the presence of the Bishop of Rome wherever he chanced to be. Its use was also prohibited in the presence of a papal legate wearing the insignia of apostolic dignity.[12]

Canon 5 also recognized for patriarchs the right of receiving judicial appeals from all the provinces within their jurisdiction

---

[10] *Supra,* p. 85.

[11] Canon 5: ". . . postquam antistites earum a Romano Pontifice receperint pallium, quod est plenitudinis officii pontificalis insigne, praestito sibi fidelitatis et obedientiae juramento, licenter et ipsi suis suffraganeis pallium largiantur, recipientes pro se professionem canonicam, et pro Romana ecclesia sponsionem obedientiae ab eisdem. . . ."—c. 23, X, *de privilegiis et excessibus privilegiatorum,* V, 33; Mansi, XXII, 992.

[12] Canon 5: ". . . Dominicae vero crucis vexillum ante se faciant ubique deferri, nisi in urbe Romana, et ubicumque summus Pontifex praesens exstiterit, aut ejus legatus, utens insigniis apostolicae dignitatis. . . ."—*loc. cit.*

when this was necessary, except of course the appeals directed to the Holy See, which were to be humbly respected.[13]

Canon 30 of the IV Lateran Council stated that the patriarchs of the four Eastern sees could remove from their own subjects a reserved suspension from conferring benefices, after that suspension had been inflicted by a provincial council on prelates or chapters who, after two successive admonitions, were found guilty of conferring ecclesiastical benefices on unworthy men.[14]

---

[13] Canon 5: ". . . In omnibus autem provinciis, eorundem jurisdictioni subjectis, ad eos, quum necesse fuerit, provocetur, salvis appellationibus ad sedem apostolicam interpositis, quibus est ab omnibus humiliter deferendum." —*loc. cit.*

[14] Canon 30: ". . . Ut autem haec salubris provisio pleniorem consequatur effectum, hujusmodi suspensionis sententia praeter Romani pontificis auctoritatem aut proprii patriarchae minime relaxetur, ut in hoc quoque quatuor patriarchales sedes specialiter honorentur."—c. 29, X, *de praebendis et dignitatibus,* III, 5; Mansi, XXII, 1018.

CHAPTER VII

The Council of Florence (1439-1445)

At the Council which was transferred to Florence by Pope Eugene IV (1431-1447) in 1439 after previously having held its sessions in Basle and Ferrara, the question of the reunion of the East and the West was again treated.[1]

The Greek delegation to the Council arrived at Ferrara in March, 1438. It included about seven hundred persons. The Greek Emperor John VIII Palaeologus (1423-1448) and the Patriarch Joseph II (1416-1439) of Constantinople personally came to Ferrara to attend the Council. The Greek Patriarchs of Alexandria, Antioch, and Jerusalem were represented by legates.

In the seating arrangement at the Council, the Latins occupied one side of the cathedral of Ferrara, the Greeks the other.[2] On the Oriental side, the Patriarch of Constantinople was given first place among the Patriarchs; and immediately after him came the legates of the Oriental Patriarchs of Alexandria, Antioch, and Jerusalem in that order.[3]

---

[1] The question of reunion had been dealt with previously by the II Council of Lyons (1274).

[2] "The Greeks insisted that the Emperor be given the first and highest place in the council and that a subordinate position be assigned to the Pope. . . . After much unpleasant discussion, it was agreed that the Latins should sit on the gospel side of the cathedral with the Pope at their head on a throne elevated above all other seats, while the Greeks should sit on the epistle side with the Emperor at their head and next to him the Patriarch. . . ."—Schroeder, *General Councils,* p. 469, footnote 7.

[3] "Disputationes seu Collationes inter Latinos et Graecos in Generali Concilio Florentino habitae, et ab Andrea de Sancta Cruce . . . conscripta in modum dialogi cum Ludovico Pontano, Collatio Prima: 'In quatuor scabellis post patriarcham dispositis sequebantur archiepiscopus Heracleensis, Alexandrini Patriarchae legitimum mandatum habens, ejusque locum tenens; archiepiscopus Ephesinus patriarchae Antiocheni legatus, archiepiscopus Menesiensis Hierosolymitani patriarchae personam repraesentans.' . . ."—Mansi, XXXI B, 1436.

The same order was kept at the cathedral of Florence after the Council had been transferred to that city.[4]

One result of the Council's work for reunion was that the Greeks, after much discussion, came to agreement with the West and a union was accomplished. Pope Eugene IV (1431-1447) announced this union of the Eastern and Western Churches in his famous decree *Laetentur coeli,* solemnly read in Latin and in Greek in the cathedral at Florence on July 6, 1439.

In this decree the order among the patriarchal sees, as it had explicitly been stated by Pope Innocent III (1198-1216) more than two centuries before, was renewed.[5]

---

[4] "Collatio XV (the first at Florence, 2 mart. 1439) : 'Primo in conventu Florentiae convenientibus cunctis ordine et modo, quo Ferrariae relatum, in quo nec imperator, nec patriarcha interfuit,' . . ."—Mansi, XXXI B, 1564, cf. also *ibid.,* p. 1694.

[5] Decretum seu Definitio *"Laetentur coeli":* "Renovantes insuper ordinem traditum in canonibus, ceterorum venerabilium Patriarcharum, ut Patriarcha Constantinopolitanus secundus sit post sanctissimum Romanum pontificem, tertius vero Alexandrinus, quartus autem Antiochenus, et quintus Hierosolymitanus, salvis videlicet privilegiis omnibus et juribus eorum."—Mansi, XXXI B, 1697-1698.

CONCLUSIONS

1. In his patriarchate the Bishop of Antioch seems to have had more than a power of confirming bishops already elected and consecrated; his consent was required, and therefore he seemingly had a power of veto in virtue of which he could forbid ordination and thus render it unlawful for anyone to receive ordination except from the Bishop of Rome, and for any bishop, except the Bishop of Rome, to grant it (cf. p. 42).

2. The patriarchal rights were not exercised in the same manner everywhere. Thus the Bishop of Rome exercised his rights in Eastern Illyricum for some time at least to some extent through a permanent vicar, the Bishop of Thessalonica, while, as far as the present writer knows, the other patriarchs did not make use of permanent vicars of this kind (cf. pp. 16; 26; 55).

3. Since Alexandria was still considered the second see in 866, and since in 1215 Constantinople was considered already to have second place in virtue of an ancient privilege, which was then made explicit in canon 5 of the IV Lateran Council, Constantinople implicitly obtained this position with the approval of canon 21 of the IV Council of Constantinople (869-870) (cf. pp. 33; 64-65; 85-86).

4. The Bishop of Constantinople was explicitly given patriarchal jurisdiction as such by the IV Council of Constantinople when, in canon 17, the statement was made: "*. . . sancta synodus . . . in nova Roma . . . priscam consuetudinem decernit in omnibus conservari, . . .*" The expression *prisca consuetudo* in this canon refers to the same thing that canon 6 of the I Council of Nicaea (325) referred to when it used the expression *antiqui mores* (cf. pp. 34; 62; 68-69).

5. The jurisdiction of patriarchs was attached to the patriarchal sees in a permanent manner. Hence it was that kind of jurisdiction which today is designated as ordinary power (cf. pp. 38-39).

BIBLIOGRAPHY

Sources

Acta Apostolicae Sedis, Commentarium Officiale, Romae, 1909—.

Acta Leonis XIII, 23 vols. and an appendix, Romae, 1881-1905.

Acta Pii IX, 9 vols., Romae, 1854-1878.

Acta Sanctae Sedis, 41 vols., Romae, 1865-1908.

Annuario Pontificio, Città del Vaticano, Tipografia Poliglotta Vaticana, 1947.

Bruns, H., *Canones Apostolorum et Conciliorum Saeculorum IV, V, VI, VII,* 2 parts, Berolini, 1839.

Bullarii Romani Continuatio, 9 tomes in 14, Prati, 1840-1856.

Bullarum Diplomatum et Privilegiorum Sanctorum Pontificum Taurinensis Editio, 24 tomes in 25; tomes 1-16 and 21-24, Augustae Taurinorum, 1857-1872; tomes 17-20, Neapoli, 1882-1883.

Codex Iuris Canonici Pii X Pontificis Maximi iussu digestus Benedicti Papae XV auctoritate promulgatus, Romae: Typis Polyglottis Vaticanis, 1917.

Codex Iuris Canonici Fontes, cura Emī Petri Card. Gasparri editi, 9 vols., Romae (postea Civitate Vaticana): Typis Polyglottis Vaticanis, 1923-1939. (Vols. VII, VIII et IX ed. cura et studio Emi Iustiniani Card. Serédi.)

Codificazione Canonica Orientale, Fonti, Serie I, 13 vols., Serie II, 16 vols., *Fontes,* Series III, 3 vols., Città del Vaticano: Tipografia Polyglotta Vaticana, 1930—.

Corpus Iuris Canonici, edito Lipsiensis secunda, post Aemilii Richteri curas . . . instruxit Aemilius Friedberg, 2 vols., Lipsiae: ex Officina Bernhardi Tauchnitz, 1879-1881. Editio anastatice repetita, 1922.

Corpus Iuris Civilis, 3 vols., Vol. I, *Institutiones* recognovit Paulus Krueger, *Digesta* recognovit Theodorus Mommsen, retractavit Paulus Krueger, 15. ed.; Vol. II, *Codex Iustinianus* recognovit et retractavit Paulus Krueger, 10. ed.; Vol. III, *Novellae* recognovit Rudolfus Schoell, absolvit Gulielmus Kroll, 5. ed., Berolini: Apud Weidmannos, 1928-1929.

Enchiridion Symbolorum Definitionum et Declarationum de Rebus Fidei et Morum, Denzinger, H., Bannwart, C., and Umberg, J., 21-23. ed., Friburgi Brisgoviae: Herder & Co., 1937.

Index Sedium Titularium Archiepiscopalium et Episcopalium, Civitate Vaticana: Typis Polyglottis Vaticanis, 1933.

Jaffé, Phillipus, *Regesta Pontificum Romanorum ab condita Ecclesia ad annum post Christum natum MCXCVIII,* 2. ed., correctam et auctam auspiciis Gulielmi Wattenbach curaverunt S. Loewenfeld, F. Kaltenbrunner, P. Ewald, 2 tomes in 1 Vol., Lipsiae: 1885-1888.

Mansi, Joannes, *Sacrorum Conciliorum Nova et amplissima Collectio,* 53 vols. in 60, Florentiae, Venetiis, Parisiis, Arnhemii, Lipsiae, 1759-1927.

Monumenta Germaniae Historica, Epistolorum Tom. VI, *Epistolae Karolini Aevi,* Tom. IV, ed. E. Perels, Berolini: Apud Weidmannos, 1925.

———, *Gregorii I Papae Registrum Epistolarum,* Epistolarum tomus I (ediderunt P. Ewald et L. Hartmann), Berolini: Apud Weidmannos, 1891.

Pitra, J. B., *Iuris Ecclesiastici Graecorum Historia et Monumenta,* 2 toms., Romae, 1864-1868.

Potthast, A., *Regesta Pontificum Romanorum inde ab anno post Christum natum MCXCVIII ad annum MCCCIV,* 2 vols., Berolini, 1874-1875.

Schroeder, H., *Disciplinary Decrees of the General Councils,* St. Louis: Herder & Co., 1937.

Schwartz, E., *Acta Conciliorum Oecumenicorum,* Toms. I & II in XI vols., Berolini et Lipsiae: W. de Gruyter & Co., 1922-1938; Tom. IV, vol. II, sumptibus Caroli J. Trübner, Argentoratensis, 1924.

Synodus Sciarfensis Syrorum in Monte Libano celebrata anno 1888, Romae: S. C. de Propaganda Fide, 1896.

Turner, C., *Ecclesiae Occidentalis Monumenta Iuris Antiquissima, Canonum et Conciliorum Graecorum Interpretationes Latinae,* 2 vols. in 6 parts, Oxonii: e Typographeo Clarendoniano, 1899-1930.

Authors

Attwater, D., *The Catholic Eastern Churches,* 2. ed., Milwaukee: Bruce, 1937.

———, *The Christian Churches of the East,* Vol. I, *Churches in Communion with Rome,* Milwaukee: Bruce, 1947.

Baronius, C., *Annales Ecclesiastici,* 37 toms., Barri-Ducis, Parisiis, 1864-1883.

Benedictus XIV, *De Synodo Dioecesana,* 2. toms., 2. Parmensis ed., Parmae, 1764.

Beste, U., *Introductio in Codicem,* ed. altera, Collegeville: St. John's Abbey Press, 1944.

Bianchi di Lucca, G., *Della Potestà e della Polizia della Chiesa,* 2. vols., Torino, 1854-1857.

Bingham, J., *The Antiquities of the Christian Church,* 24 books in 2 vols., London: Henry Bohn, 1852-1867.

Bouix, D., *Institutiones Juris Canonici in Varios Tractatus Divisae, Tractatus de Episcopo,* 2. ed., 2 toms. in 1, Parisiis, Insulis, Tornaci, 1873.

Buckland, *A Textbook of Roman Law from Augustus to Justinian,* 2. ed., Cambridge: University Press, 1932.

Cappello, F., *Summa Iuris Canonici,* 3. vols., Romae: Apud Aedes Pontificiae Universitatis Gregorianae; Vols. 1 & II, 4. ed., 1945; Vol. III, ed. altera, 1940.

Catholic Encyclopedia, The, 15. vols., Index and 2 Supplements, New York: Robert Appleton Co., 1907-1922.

Cicognani, A., *Canon Law,* 2. revised ed. Westminster: The Newman Bookshop, 1947.

Coronata, Matthaeus Conte a, *Institutiones Iuris Canonici,* 5 vols., ed. altera, Taurini: Marietti, 1939-1947.

Devoti, J., *Institutionum Canonicarum Libri IV,* 4. ed., Veneta juxta v. Romanam, 3 toms., Venetiis, 1827.

Eidenschink, J., *The Election of Bishops in the Letters of Gregory the Great,* The Catholic University of America Canon Law Studies, n. 215, Washington, D. C.: The Catholic University of America Press, 1945.

Fortescue, A., *The Lesser Eastern Churches,* London: Catholic Truth Society, 1913.

———, *The Uniate Eastern Churches,* ed. G. Smith, New York, Cincinnati, Chicago: Benziger Brothers, 1923.

Funk, Francis X., *A Manual of Church History,* translated from the German by P. Perciballi and edited by W. H. Kent, 2 vols., London: Burns, Oates and Washbourne, Ltd., 1938.

Gams, P., *Series Episcoporum Ecclesiae Catholicae,* Ratisbonae, 1873.

Grisar, H., *History of Rome and the Popes in the Middle Ages,* 3 vols., edition of Cappadelta, London: Kegan Paul, Trench, Trübner & Co., Ltd., 1911-1912.

Hefele, K., and Leclercq, H., *Histoire des Conciles,* 10 vols. in 19, Paris: Letouzey and Ané, 1907-1938.

Heimbucher, M., *Die Orden und Kongregationen der Katholischen Kirche,* 3. ed., 2 vols., Paderborn: Schöningh, 1933-1934.

Hergenröther, J., *Photius, Patriarch von Constantinopel,* 3 vols., Regensburg, 1867-1869.

Hickey, J., *Summula Philosophiae Scholasticae,* 3 vols., Dublini: Apud Browne et Nolan; Vol. I, ed. altera, 1908; Vol. II, 1904; Vol. III, pars prior, 1905.

Janin, R., *The Separated Eastern Churches,* trans. by P. Boylan, St. Louis: Herder Book Co., 1933.

Kurtscheid, B., *Historia Iuris Canonici, Historia Institutorum,* Vol. I, *Ab Ecclesiae Fundatione usque ad Gratianum,* Romae: Officium Libri Catholici, 1941.

Laux, J., *Church History,* New York: Benziger Brothers, Inc., 1932.

Le Quien, M., *Oriens Christianus, in Quattuor Patriarchatus Digestus,* 3 toms., Parisiis, 1740.

Mamachi, T. M., *Origines et Antiquitates Christianae,* ed. altera, 6 vols., Romae, 1842-1851.

Marbach, J., *Marriage Legislation for the Catholics of the Oriental Rites in the United States and Canada,* The Catholic University of America Canon Law Studies, n. 243, Washington, D. C.: The Catholic University of America Press, 1946.

Migne, J. P., *Patrologiae Cursus Completus, Series Graeca,* 161 vols., Parisiis, 1856-1866.

———, *Patrologiae Cursus Completus, Series Latina,* 221 vols., Parisiis, 1844-1864.

Moroni, G., *Dizionario di Erudizione Storico-Ecclesiastica da S. Pietro sino ai Nostri Giorni,* 103 vols. & 6 vols. Indicis, Venezia, 1840-1879.

Petrani, A., *De Relatione Iuridica inter Diversos Ritus in Ecclesia Catholica,* Romae: Marietti, 1930.

Sägmuller, J. B., *Lehrbuch des katholischen Kirchenrechts,* 4. ed., 1 vol. in 4 parts, Freiburg im Breisgau: Herder & Co., G. M. B. H. Verlagsbuchhandlung, 1925-1934.

Tanquerey, A., *Synopsis Theologiae Dogmaticae,* 24. ed., 3 toms.; Tom. I, Tornaci (Belg.), 1937; Tom. II, Parisiis, 1933; Tom. III, Parisiis, 1938.

Thomassinus, L., *Vetus et Nova Ecclesiae Disciplina circa Beneficia et Beneficiarios,* 3 parts in 10, Magontiaci, 1787.

Van Hove, A., *Commentarium Lovaniense in Codicem Iuris Canonici,* Vol. I, tom. I (*Prolegomena*), ed. altera, Mechliniae-Romae: Dessain, 1945.

Vermeersch, A., and Creusen, J., *Epitome Iuris Canonici,* 6. ed., 3 toms., Mechliniae-Romae: Dessain, 1937-1946.

Wernz, F., and Vidal, P., *Ius Canonicum,* 7 toms. in 9, Romae: Universitas Gregoriana, 1927-1946, Tom. I, 1938; Tom. II, 3. ed., a P. Philippo Aguirre recognita, 1943; Tom. III, 1933; Tom. IV, Pars I, 1934; Tom. IV, Pars II, 1935; Tom. V, 3. ed., a P. Philippo Aguirre recognita, 1946; Tom. VI, 1927; Tom. VI, Pars altera, 1928; Tom. VII, 1937.

Articles

Fortescue, A., "Patriarch and Patriarchate,"—*Catholic Encyclopedia,* XI, 549-553.

Kirsch, J. P., "Nicholas I, Saint, Pope,"—*Catholic Encyclopedia,* XI, 54-55.

Woods, J. M., "Alexandria, The Church of,"—*Catholic Encyclopedia,* I, 300-302.

BIOGRAPHICAL NOTE

Thomas Aloysius Kane was born in Philadelphia, Pa., on May 28, 1915. After completing his elementary school education at the Most Precious Blood of Our Lord Parochial School of that city in 1929, he attended Roman Catholic High School and La Salle College in the same city, and received the degree of Bachelor of Science in June, 1937. In September, 1937, he started his studies for the Sacred Priesthood at St. Charles Borromeo Seminary, Overbrook, Pa., where he received the degree of Bachelor of Arts in 1941. He was ordained to the Sacred Priesthood at Philadelphia on June 3, 1944. After his ordination he was appointed assistant pastor at St. Joseph's Church, Girardville, Pa., where he remained until his appointment to graduate studies in Canon Law at the Catholic University of America. He was admitted to the School of Canon Law at the Catholic University in the fall of 1945. In June, 1946, he was given the Baccalaureate in Canon Law; and in June, 1947, the Licentiate in Canon Law.

INDEX

CANON LAW STUDIES*

1. Freriks, Rev. Celestine A., C.PP.S., J.C.D., Religious Congregations in Their External Relations, 121 pp., 1916.
2. Galliher, Rev. Daniel M., O.P., J.C.D., Canonical Elections, 117 pp., 1917.
3. Borkowski, Rev. Aurelius L., O.F.M., J.C.D., De Confraternitatibus Ecclesiasticis, 136 pp., 1918.
4. Castillo, Rev. Cayo, J.C.D., Disertacion Historico-Canonica sobre la Potestad del Cabildo en Sede Vacante o Impedida del Vicario Capitular, 99 pp., 1919 (1918).
5. Kubelbeck, Rev. William J., S.T.B., J.C.D., The Sacred Penitentiaria and Its Relation to Faculties of Ordinaries and Priests, 129 pp., 1918.
6. Petrovits, Rev. Joseph J. C., S.T.D., J.C.D., The New Church Law on Matrimony, X-461 pp., 1919.
7. Hickey, Rev. John J., S.T.B., J.C.D., Irregularities and Simple Impediments in the New Code of Canon Law, 100 pp., 1920.
8. Klekotka, Rev. Peter J., S.T.B., J.C.D., Diocesan Consultors, 179 pp., 1920.
9. Wanenmacher, Rev. Francis, J.C.D., The Evidence in Ecclesiastical Procedure Affecting the Marriage Bond, 1920 (Printed 1935).
10. Golden, Rev. Henry Francis, J.C.D., Parochial Benefices in the New Code, IV-119 pp., 1921 (Printed 1925).
11. Koudelka, Rev. Charles J., J.C.D., Pastors, Their Rights and Duties According to the New Code of Canon Law, 211 pp., 1921.
12. Melo, Rev. Antonius, O.F.M., J.C.D., De Exemptione Regularium, X-188 pp., 1921.
13. Schaaf, Rev. Valentine Theodore, O.F.M., S.T.B., J.C.D., The Cloister, X-180 pp., 1921.
14. Burke, Rev. Thomas Joseph, S.T.D., J.C.D., Competence in Ecclesiastical Tribunals, IV-117 pp., 1922.
15. Leech, Rev. George Leo, J.C.D., A Comparative Study of the Constitution "Apostolicae Sedis" and the "Codex Juris Canonici," 179 pp., 1922.
16. Motry, Rev. Hubert Louis, S.T.D., J.C.D., Diocesan Faculties According to the Code of Canon Law, II-167 pp., 1922.
17. Murphy, Rev. George Lawrence, J.C.D., Delinquencies and Penalties in the Administration and the Reception of the Sacraments, IV-121 pp., 1923.

***All published numbers are available from the Catholic University of America Press, 621 Michigan Avenue, N.E., Washington 17, D. C., except the following: Numbers 1-114 inclusive, and numbers 116, 118, 120, 122, 123, 136, 162 and 198.**

18. O'Reilly, Rev. John Anthony, S.T.B., J.C.D., Ecclesiastical Sepulture in the New Code of Canon Law, II-129 pp., 1923.
19. Michalicka, Rev. Wenceslas Cyril, O.S.B., J.C.D., Judicial Procedure in Dismissal of Clerical Exempt Religious, 107 pp., 1923.
20. Dargin, Rev. Edward Vincent, S.T.B., J.C.D., Reserved Cases According to the Code of Canon Law, IV-103 pp., 1924.
21. Godfrey, Rev. John A., S.T.B., J.C.D., The Right of Patronage According to the Code of Canon Law, 153 pp., 1924.
22. Hagedorn, Rev. Francis Edward, J.C.D., General Legislation on Indulgences, II-154 pp., 1924.
23. King, Rev. James Ignatius, J.C.D., The Administration of the Sacraments to Dying Non-Catholics, V-141 pp., 1924.
24. Winslow, Rev. Francis Joseph, M.M., J.C.D., Vicars and Prefects Apostolic, IV-149 pp., 1924.
25. Correa, Rev. Jose Servelion, S.T.L., J.C.D., La Potestad Legislativa de la Iglesia Catolica, IV-127 pp., 1925.
26. Dugan, Rev. Henry Francis, A.M., J.C.D., The Judiciary Department of the Diocesan Curia, 87 pp., 1925.
27. Keller, Rev. Charles Frederick, S.T.B., J.C.D., Mass Stipends, 167 pp., 1925.
238. Paschang, Rev. John Linus, J.C.D., The Sacramentals According to the Code of Canon Law, 129 pp., 1925.
29. Piontek, Rev. Cyrillus, O.F.M., S.T.B., J.C.D., De Indulto Exclaustrationis necnon Saecularizationis, XIII-289 pp., 1925.
30. Kearney, Rev. Richard Joseph, S.T.B., J.C.D., Sponsors at Baptism According to the Code of Canon Law, IV-127 pp. 1925.
31. Bartlett, Rev. Chester Joseph, A.M., LL.B., J.C.D., The Tenure of Parochial Property in the United States of America, V-108 pp., 1926.
32. Kilker, Rev. Adrian Jerome, J.C.D., Extreme Unction, V-425 pp., 1926.
33. McCormick, Rev. Robert Emmett, J.C.D., Confessors of Religious, VIII-266 pp., 1926.
34. Miller, Rev. Newton Thomas, J.C.D., Founded Masses According to the Code of Canon Law, VII-93 pp., 1926.
35. Roelker, Rev. Edward G., S.T.D., J.C.D., Principles of Privilege According to the Code of Canon Law, XI-166 pp., 1926.
36. Bakalarczyk, Rev. Richardus, M.I.C., J.U.D., De Novitiatu, VIII-208 pp., 1927.
37. Pizzuti, Rev. Lawrence, O.F.M., J.U.L., De Parochis Religiosis, 1927. (Not Printed.)
38. Bliley, Rev. Nicholas Martin, O.S.B., J.C.D., Altars According to the Code of Canon Law, XIX-132 pp., 1927.
39. Brown, Mr. Brendan Francis, A.B., LL.M., J.U.D., The Canonical Juristic Personality with Special Reference to its Status in the United States of America, V-212 pp., 1927.

40. Cavanaugh, Rev. William Thomas, C.P., J.U.D., The Reservation of the Blessed Sacrament, VIII-101 pp., 1927.
41. Doheny, Rev. William J., C.S.C., A.B., J.U.D., Church Property: Modes of Acquisition, X-118 pp., 1927.
42. Feldhaus, Rev. Aloysius H., C.PP.S., J.C.D., Oratories, IX-141 pp., 1927.
43. Kelly, Rev. James Patrick, A.B., J.C.D., The Jurisdiction of the Simple Confessor, X-208 pp., 1927.
44. Neuberger, Rev. Nicholas J., J.C.D., Canon 6 or the Relation of the Codex Juris Canonici to the Preceding Legislation, V-95 pp., 1927.
45. O'Keefe, Rev. Gerald Michael, J.C.D., Matrimonial Dispensations, Powers of Bishops, Priests, and Confessors, VIII-232 pp., 1927.
46. Quigley, Rev. Joseph, A.M., A.B., J.C.D., Condemned Societies, 139 pp., 1927.
47. Zaplotnik, Rev. Johannes Leo, J.C.D., De Vicariis Foraneis, X-142 pp., 1927.
48. Duskie, Rev. John Aloysius, A.B., J.C.D., The Canonical Status of the Orientals in the United States, VIII-196 pp., 1928.
49. Hyland, Rev. Francis Edward, J.C.D., Excommunication, Its Nature, Historical Development and Effects, VIII-181 pp., 1928.
50. Reinmann, Rev. Gerald Joseph, O.M.C., J.C.D., The Third Order Secular of Saint Francis, 201 pp., 1928.
51. Schenk, Rev. Francis J., J.C.D., The Matrimonial Impediments of Mixed Religion and Disparity of Cult, XVI-318 pp., 1929.
52. Coady, Rev. John Joseph, S.T.D., J.U.D., A.M., The Appointment of Pastors, VIII-150 pp., 1929.
53. Kay, Rev. Thomas Henry, J.C.D., Competence in Matrimonial Procedure, VIII-164 pp., 1929.
54. Turner, Rev. Sidney Joseph, C.P., J.U.D., The Vow of Poverty, XLIX-217 pp., 1929.
55. Kearney, Rev. Raymond A., A.B., S.T.D., J.C.D., The Principles of Delegation, VII-149 pp., 1929.
56. Conran, Rev. Edward James, A.B., J.C.D., The Interdict, V-163 pp., 1930.
57. O'Neill, Rev. William H., J.C.D., Papal Rescripts of Favor, VII-218 pp., 1930.
58. Bastnagel, Rev. Clement Vincent, J.U.D., The Appointment of Parochial Adjutants and Assistants, XV-257 pp., 1930.
59. Ferry, Rev. William A., A.B., J.C.D., Stole Fees, V-136 pp., 1930.
60. Costello, Rev. John Michael, A.B., J.C.D., Domicile and Quasi-Domicile, VII-201 pp., 1930.
61. Kremer, Rev. Michael Nicholas, A.B., S.T.B., J.C.D., Church Support in the United States, VI-136 pp., 1930.
62. Angulo, Rev. Luis, C.M., J.C.D., Legislation de la Iglesia sobre la intencion en la application de la Santa Misa, VII-104 pp., 1931.

63. Frey, Rev. Wolfgang Norbert, O.S.B., A.B., J.C.D., The Act of Religious Profession, VIII-174 pp., 1931.
64. Roberts, Rev. James Brendan, A.B., J.C.D., The Banns of Marriage, XIV-140 pp., 1931.
65. Ryder, Rev. Raymond Aloysius, A.B., J.C.D., Simony, IX-151 pp., 1931.
66. Campagna, Rev. Angelo, Ph.D., J.U.D., Il Vicario Generale del Vescovo, VII-205 pp., 1931.
67. Cox, Rev. Joseph Godfrey, A.B., J.C.D., The Administration of Seminaries, VI-124 pp., 1931.
68. Gregory, Rev. Donald J., J.U.D., The Pauline Privilege, XV-165 pp., 1931.
69. Donohue, Rev. John F., J.C.D., The Impediment of Crime, VII-110 pp., 1931.
70. Dooley, Rev. Eugene A., O.M.I., J.C.D., Church Law on Sacred Relics, IX-143 pp., 1931.
71. Orth, Rev. Clement Raymond, O.M.C., J.C.D., The Approbation of Religious Institutes, 171 pp., 1931.
72. Pernicone, Rev. Joseph M., A.B., J.C.D., The Ecclesiastical Prohibition of Books, XII-267 pp., 1932.
73. Clinton, Rev. Connell, A.B., J.C.D., The Paschal Precept, IX-108 pp., 1932.
74. Donnelly, Rev. Francis B., A.M., S.T.L., J.C.D., The Diocesan Synod, VIII-125 pp., 1932.
75. Torrente, Rev. Camilo, C.M.F., J.C.D., Las Procesiones Sagradas, V-145 pp., 1932.
76. Murphy, Rev. Edwin J., C.PP.S., J.C.D., Suspension Ex Informata Conscientia, XI-122 pp., 1932.
77. MacKenzie, Rev. Eric F., A.M., S.T.L., J.C.D., The Delict of Heresy in its Commission, Penalization, Absolution, VII-124 pp., 1932.
78. Lyons, Rev. Avitus E., S.T.B., J.C.D., The Collegiate Tribunal of First Instance, XI-147 pp., 1932.
79. Connolly, Rev. Thomas A., J.C.D., Appeals, XI-195 pp., 1932.
80. Sangmeister, Rev. Joseph V., A.B., J.C.D., Force and Fear as Precluding Matrimonial Consent, V-211 pp., 1932.
81. Jaeger, Rev. Leo A., A.B., J.C.D., The Administration of Vacant and Quasi-Vacant Episcopal Sees in the United States, IX-229 pp., 1932.
82. Rimlinger, Rev. Herbert T., J.C.D., Error Invalidating Matrimonial Consent, VII-79 pp., 1932.
83. Barrett, Rev. John D. M., S.S., J.C.D., A Comparative Study of the Third Plenary Council of Baltimore and the Code, IX-221 pp., 1932.
84. Carberry, Rev. John J., Ph.D., S.T.D., J.C.D., The Juridical Form of Marriage, X-177 pp., 1934.
85. Dolan, Rev. John L., A.B., J.C.D., The Defensor Vinculi, XII-157 pp., 1934.

86. HANNAN, REV. JEROME D., A.M., S.T.D., LL.B., J.C.D., The Canon Law of Wills, IX-517 pp., 1934.
87. LEMIEUX, REV. DELISE A., A.M., J.C.D., The Sentence in Ecclesiastical Procedure, IX-131 pp., 1934.
88. O'ROURKE, REV. JAMES J., A.B., J.C.D., Parish Registers, VII-109 pp.. 1934.
89. TIMLIN, REV. BARTHOLOMEW, O.F.M., A.M., J.C.D., Conditional Matrimonial Consent, X-381 pp., 1934.
90. WAHL, REV. FRANCIS X., A.B., J.C.D., The Matrimonial Impediments of Consanguinity and Affinity, VI-125 pp., 1934.
91. WHITE, REV. ROBERT J., A.B., LL.B., S.T.B., J.C.D., Canonical Ante-Nuptial Promises and the Civil Law, VI-152 pp., 1934.
92. HERRERA, REV. ANTONIO PARRA, O.C.D., J.C.D., Legislacion Ecclesiastica sobra el Ayuno y la Abstinencia, XI-191 pp., 1935.
93. KENNEDY, REV. EDWIN J., J.C.D., The Special Matrimonial Process in Cases of Evident Nullity, X-165 pp., 1935.
94. MANNING, REV. JOHN J., A.B., J.C.D., Presumption of Law in Matrimonial Procedure, XI-111 pp., 1935.
95. MOEDER, REV. JOHN M., J.C.D., The Proper Bishop for Ordination and Dimissorial Letters, VII-135 pp., 1935.
96. O'MARA, REV. WILLIAM A., A.B., J.C.D., Canonical Causes for Matrimonial Dispensations, IX-155 pp., 1935.
97. REILLY, REV. PETER, J.C.D., Residence of Pastors, IX-81 pp., 1935.
98. SMITH, REV. MARINER T., O.P., S.T.Lr., J.C.D., The Penal Law for Religious, VII-169 pp., 1935.
99. WHALEN, REV. DONALD W., A.M., J.C.D., The Value of Testimonial Evidence in Matrimonial Procedure, XIII-297 pp., 1935.
100. CLEARY, REV. JOSEPH F., J.C.D., Canonical Limitations on the Alienation of Church Property, VIII-141 pp., 1936.
101. GLYNN, REV. JOHN C., J.C.D., The Promoter of Justice, XX-337 pp., 1936.
102. BRENNAN, REV. JAMES H., S.S., M.A., S.T.B., J.C.D., The Simple Convalidation of Marriage, VI-135 pp., 1937.
103. BRUNINI, REV. JOSEPH BERNARD, J.C.D., The Clerical Obligations of Canons 139 and 142, X-121 pp., 1937.
104. CONNOR, REV. MAURICE, A.B., J.C.D., The Administrative Removal of Pastors, VIII-159 pp., 1937.
105. GUILFOYLE, REV. MERLIN JOSEPH, J.C.D., Custom, XI-144 pp., 1937.
106. HUGHES, REV. JAMES AUSTIN, A.B., A.M., J.C.D., Witnesses in Criminal Trials of Clerics, IX-140 pp., 1937.
107. JANSEN, REV. RAYMOND J., A.B., S.T.L., J.C.D., Canonical Provisions for Catechetical Instruction, VII-153 pp., 1937.
108. KEALY, REV. JOHN JAMES, A.B., J.C.D., The Introductory Libellus in Church Court Procedure, XI-131 pp., 1937.

109. McManus, Rev. James Edward, C.Ss.R., J.C.D., The Administration of Temporal Goods in Religious Institutes, XVI-196 pp., 1937.
110. Moriarty, Rev. Eugene James, J.C.D., Oaths in Ecclesiastical Courts, X-115 pp., 1937.
111. Rainer, Rev. Eligius George, C.Ss.R., J.C.D., Suspension of Clerics, XVII-249 pp., 1937.
112. Reilly, Rev. Thomas F., C.Ss.R., J.C.D., Visitation of Religious, VI-195 pp., 1938.
113. Moriarity, Rev. Francis E., C.Ss.R., J.C.D., The Extraordinary Absolution from Censures, XV-334 pp., 1938.
114. Connolly, Rev. Nicholas P., J.C.D., The Canonical Erection of Parishes, X-132 pp., 1938.
115. Donovan, Rev. James Joseph, J.C.D., The Pastor's Obligation in Prenuptial Investigation, XII-322 pp., 1938.
116. Harrigan, Rev. Robert J., M.A., S.T.B., J.C.D., The Radical Sanation of Invalid Marriages, VIII-208 pp., 1938.
117. Boffa, Rev. Conrad Humbert, J.C.D., Canonical Provisions for Catholic Schools, VII-211 pp., 1939.
118. Parsons, Rev. Anscar John, O.M.Cap., J.C.D., Canonical Elections, XII-236 pp., 1939.
119. Reilly, Rev. Edward Michael, A.B., J.C.D., The General Norms of Dispensation, XII-156 pp., 1939.
120. Ryan, Rev. Gerald Aloysius, A.B., J.C.D., Principles of Episcopal Jurisdiction, XIII-172 pp., 1939.
121. Burton, Rev. Francis James, C.S.C., A.B., J.C.D., A Commentary on Canon 1125, X-222 pp., 1940.
122. Miaskiewicz, Rev. Francis Sigismund, J.C.D., Supplied Jurisdiction According to Canon 209, XII-340 pp., 1940.
123. Rice, Rev. Patrick William, A.B., J.C.D., Proof of Death in Prenuptial Investigation, VIII-156 pp., 1940.
124. Anglin, Rev. Thomas Francis, M.S., J.C.D., The Eucharistic Fast, VIII-183 pp., 1941.
125. Coleman, Rev. John Jerome, J.C.D., The Minister of Confirmation, VI-153 pp., 1941.
126. Downs, Rev. Joseph Emmanuel, A.B., J.C.D., The Concept of Clerical Immunity, XI-163 pp., 1941.
127. Esswein, Rev. Anthony Albert, J.C.D., Extrajudicial Penal Powers of Ecclesiastical Superiors, X-144 pp., 1941.
128. Farrell, Rev. Benjamin Francis, M.A., S.T.L., J.C.D., The Rights and Duties of the Local Ordinary Regarding Congregations of Women Religious of Pontifical Approval, V-195 pp., 1941.
129. Feeney, Rev. Thomas John, A.B., S.T.L., J.C.D., Restitutio in Integrum, VI-169 pp., 1941.
130. Findlay, Rev. Stephen William, O.S.B., A.B., J.C.D., Canonical Norms Governing the Deposition and Degradation of Clerics, XVII-279 pp., 1941.

131. Goodwine, Rev. John, A.B., S.T.L., J.C.D., The Right of the Church to Acquire Property, VIII-119 pp., 1941.
132. Heston, Rev. Edward Louis, C.S.C., Ph.D., S.T.D., J.C.D., The Alienation of Church Property in the United States, XII-222 pp., 1941.
133. Hogan, Rev. James John, A.B., S.T.L., J.C.D., Judicial Advocates and Procurators, XIII-200 pp., 1941.
134. Kealy, Rev. Thomas M., A.B., Litt.D., J.C.D., Dowry of Women Religious, IX-152 pp., 1941.
135. Keene, Rev. Michael James, O.S.B., J.C.D., Religious Ordinaries and Canon 198, V-164 pp., 1942.
136. Kerin, Rev. Charles A., S.S., M.A., S.T.B., J.C.D., The Privation of Christian Burial, XVI-279 pp., 1941.
137. Louis, Rev. William Francis, M.A., J.C.D., Diocesan Archives, X-101 pp., 1941.
138. McDevitt, Rev. Gilbert Joseph, A.B., J.C.D., Legitimacy and Legitimation, X-247 pp., 1941.
139. McDonough, Rev. Thomas Joseph, A.B., J.C.D., Apostolic Administrators, X-217 pp., 1941.
140. Meier, Rev. Carl Anthony, A.B., J.C.D., Penal Administrative Procedure Against Negligent Pastors, XI-240 pp., 1941.
141. Schmidt, Rev. John Rogg, A.B., J.C.D., The Principles of Authentic Interpretation in Canon 17 of the Code of Canon Law, XII-331 pp., 1941.
142. Slafkosky, Rev. Andrew Leonard, A.B., J.C.D., The Canonical Episcopal Visitation of the Diocese, X-197 pp., 1941.
143. Swoboda, Rev. Innocent Robert, O.F.M., J.C.D., Ignorance in Relation to the Imputability of Delicts, IX-271 pp., 1941.
144. Dube, Rev. Arthur Joseph, A.B., J.C.D., The General Principles for the Reckoning of Time in Canon Law, VIII-299 pp., 1941.
145. McBride, Rev. James T., A.B., J.C.D., Incardination and Excardination of Seculars, XX-585 pp., 1941.
146. Krol, Rev. John T., J.C.D., The Defendant in Ecclesiastical Trials, XII-207 pp., 1942.
147. Comyns, Rev. Joseph J., C.Ss.R., A.B., J.C.D., Papal and Episcopal Administration of Church Property, XIV-155 pp., 1942.
148. Barry, Rev. Garrett Francis, O.M.I., J.C.D., Violation of the Cloister, XII-260 pp., 1942.
149. Bolduc, Rev. Gatien, C.S.V., A.B., S.T.L., J.C.D., Les Etudes dans les Religions Clericales, VIII-155 pp., 1942.
150. Boyles, Rev. David John, M.A., J.C.D., The Juridic Effects of Moral Certitude on Pre-Nuptial Guarantees, XII-188 pp., 1942.
151. Canavan, Rev. Walter Joseph, M.A., Litt.D., J.C.D., The Profession of Faith, XII-143 pp., 1942.
152. Desrochers, Rev. Bruno, A.B., Ph.L., S.T.B., J.C.D., Le Premier Concile Plenier de Quebec et le Code de Droit Canonique, XIV-186 pp., 1942.

153. Dillon, Rev. Robert Edward, A.B., J.C.D., Common Law Marriage, X-148 pp., 1942.
154. Dodwell, Rev. Edward John, Ph.D., S.T.B., J.C.D., The Time and Place for the Celebration of Marriage, X-156 pp., 1942.
155. Donnellan, Rev. Thomas Andrew, A.B., J.C.D., The Obligation of the Missa pro Populo, VII-131 pp., 1942.
156. Eltz, Rev. Louis Anthony, A.B., J.C.D., Cooperation in Crime, XII-208 pp., 1942.
157. Gass, Rev. Sylvester Francis, M.A., J.C.D., Ecclesiastical Pensions, XI-206 pp., 1942.
158. Guiniven, Rev. John Joseph, C.Ss.R., J.C.D., The Precept of Hearing Mass, XIV-188 pp., 1942.
159. Gulczynski, Rev. John Theophilus, J.C.D., The Desecration and Violation of Churches, X-126 pp., 1942.
160. Hammill, Rev. John Leo, M.A., J.C.D., The Obligations of the Traveler According to Canon 14, VIII-204 pp., 1942.
161. Haydt, Rev. John Joseph, A.B., J.C.D., Reserved Benefices, XI-148 pp., 1942.
162. Huser, Rev. Roger John, O.F.M., A.B., J.C.D., The Crime of Abortion in Canon Law, XII-187 pp., 1942.
163. Kearney, Rev. Francis Patrick, A.B., S.T.L., J.C.D., The Principles of Canon 1127, X-162 pp., 1942.
164. Linahen, Rev. Leo James, S.T.L., J.C.D., De Absolutione Complicis in Peccato Turpi, 114 pp., 1942.
165. McCloskey, Rev. Joseph Aloysius, A.B., J.C.D., The Subject of Ecclesiastical Law According to Canon 12, XVII-246 pp., 1942.
166. O'Neill, Rev. Francis Joseph, C.Ss.R., J.C.D., The Dismissal of Religious in Temporary Vows, XIII-220 pp., 1942.
167. Prince, Rev. John Edward, A.B., S.T.D., J.C.D., The Diocesan Chancellor, X-136 pp., 1942.
168. Riesner, Rev. Albert Joseph, C.Ss.R., J.C.D., Apostates and Fugitives from Religious Institutes, IX-168 pp., 1942.
169. Stenger, Rev. Joseph Bernard, J.C.D., The Mortgaging of Church Property, 186 pp., 1942.
170. Waldron, Rev. Joseph Francis, A.B., J.C.D., The Minister of Baptism, XII-197 pp., 1942.
171. Willett, Rev. Robert Albert, J.C.D., The Probative Value of Documents in Ecclesiastical Trials, X-124 pp., 1942.
172. Woeber, Rev. Edward Martin, M.A., J.C.D., The Interpellations, XII-161 pp., 1942.
173. Benko, Rev. Matthew Aloysius, O.S.B., M.A., J.C.D., The Abbot Nullius, XIV-148 pp., 1943.
174. Christ, Rev. Joseph James, M.A., S.T.L., J.C.D., Dispensation from Vindicative Penalties, XIV-285 pp., 1943.

175. Clancy, Rev. Patrick M. J., O.P., A.B., S.T.Lr., J.C.D., The Local Religious Superior, X-299 pp., 1943.
176. Clarke, Rev. Thomas James, J.C.D., Parish Societies, XII-147 pp., 1943.
177. Connolly, Rev. John Patrick, S.T.L., J.C.D., Synodal Examiners and Parish Priest Consultors, X-223 pp., 1943.
178. Drumm, Rev. William Martin, A.B., J.C.D., Hospital Chaplains, XII-175 pp., 1943.
179. Flanagan, Rev. Bernard Joseph, A.B., S.T.L., J.C.D., The Canonical Erection of Religious Houses, X-147 pp., 1943.
180. Kelleher, Rev. Stephen Joseph, A.B., S.T.B., J.C.D., Discussions with non-Catholics; Canonical Legislation, X-93 pp., 1943.
181. Lewis, Rev. Gordian, C.P., J.C.D., Chapters in Religious Institutes, XII-169 pp., 1943.
182. Marx, Rev. Adolph, J.C.D., The Declaration of Nullity of Marriages Contracted Outside the Church, X-151 pp., 1943.
183. Matulenas, Rev. Raymond Anthony, O.S.B., A.B., J.C.D., Communication a Source of Privileges, XII-225 pp., 1943.
184. O'Leary, Rev. Charles Gerard, C.Ss.R., J.C.D., Religious Dismissed After Perpetual Profession, X-213 pp., 1943.
185. Power, Rev. Cornelius Michael, J.C.D., The Blessing of Cemeteries, XII-231 pp., 1943.
186. Shuhler, Rev. Ralph Vincent, O.S.A., J.C.D., Privileges of Regulars to Absolve and Dispense, XII-195 pp., 1943.
187. Ziolkowski, Rev. Thaddeus Stanislaus, A.B., J.C.D., The Consecration and Blessing of Churches, XII-131 pp., 1943.
188. Heneghan, Rev. John Joseph, S.T.D., J.C.D., The Marriages of Unworthy Catholics: Canons 1065 and 1066, XVI-213 pp., 1944.
189. Carroll, Rev. Coleman Francis, M.C., S.T.L., J.C.L., Charitable Institutions.
190. Cieslük, Rev. Joseph Edward, Ph.B., S.T.L., J.C.D., National Parishes in the United States, VI-178 pp., 1944.
191. Coburn, Rev. Vincent Paul, A.B., J.C.D., Marriages of Conscience, XII-172 pp., 1944.
192. Connors, Rev. Charles Paul, C.S.Sp., A.B., J.C.D., Extra-Judicial Procurators in the Code of Canon Law, X-94 pp., 1944.
193. Coyle, Rev. Paul Raymond, A.B., J.C.D., Judicial Exceptions, X-142 pp., 1944.
194. Fair, Rev. Bartholomew Francis, A.B., S.T.L., J.C.D., The Impediment of Abduction, XII-122 pp., 1944.
195. Gallagher, Rev. Thomas Raphael, O.P., A.B., S.T.Lr., J.C.D., The Examination of the Qualities of the Ordinand, X-166 pp., 1944.
196. Gannon, Rev. John Mark, S.T.L., J.C.D., The Interstices Required for the Promotion to Orders, XII-100 pp., 1944.

197. Goldsmith, Rev. J. William, B.C.S., S.T.L., J.C.D., The Competence of Church and State over Marriage—Disputed Points, X-128 pp., 1944.
198. Goodwine, Rev. Joseph Gerard, A.B., S.T.B., J.C.D., The Reception of Converts, XIV-326 pp., 1944.
199. Kowalski, Rev. Romuald Eugene, O.F.M., A.B., J.C.D., Sustenance of Religious Houses of Regulars, X-174 pp., 1944.
200. McCoy, Rev. Alan Edward, O.F.M., J.C.D., Force and Fear in Relation to Delictual Imputability and Penal Responsibility, XII-160 pp., 1944.
201. McDevitt, Rev. Vincent John, Ph.B., S.T.L., J.C.L., Perjury.
202. Martin, Rev. Thomas Owen, Ph.D., S.T.D., J.C.D., Adverse possession, Prescription and Limitation of Actions; The Canonical "Praescriptio," XX-208 pp., 1944.
203. Miklosovic, Rev Paul John, A.B., J.C.L., Attempted Marriages and Their Consequent Juridic Effects.
204. Mundy, Rev. Thomas Maurice, A.B., S.T.L., J.C.D., The Union of Parishes, X-164 pp., 1944.
205. O'Dea, Rev. John Coyle, A.B., J.C.D., The Matrimonial Impediment of Nonage, VIII-126 pp., 1944.
206. Olalia, Rev. Alexander Ayson, S.T.L., J.C.D., A Comparative Study of the Christian Constitution of States and the Constitution of the Philippine Commonwealth, XII-136 pp., 1944.
207. Poisson, Rev. Pierre-Marie, C.S.C., A.B., Ph.L., Th.L., J.C.L., Droits Patrimoniaux des Maisons et des Eglises Religieuses.
208. Stadalnikas, Rev. Casimir Joseph, M.I.C., J.C.D., Reservation of Censures, X-141 pp., 1944.
209. Sullivan, Rev. Eugene Henry, S.T.L., J.C.D., Proof of the Reception of the Sacraments, X-165 pp., 1944.
210. Vaughan, Rev. William Edward, J.C.D., Constitutions for Diocesan Courts, X-210 pp., 1944.
211. Paro, Rev. Gin, S.T.D., J.C.L., The Right of Apostolic Legation.
212. Balzer, Rev. Ralph Francis, C.P., J.C.D., The Computation of Time in a Canonical Novitiate, X-227 pp., 1945.
213. Dougherty, Rev. John Whelan, A.B., S.T.L., J.C.D., De Inquisitione Speciali, XII-195 pp., 1945.
214. Dziob, Rev. Michael Walter, J.C.D., The Sacred Congregation for the Oriental Church, XII-181 pp., 1945.
215. Eidenschink, Rev. John Albert, O.S.B., B.A., J.C.D., The Election of Bishops in the Letters of Pope Gregory the Great, VIII-200 pp., 1945.
216. Gill, Rev. Nicholas, C.P., J.C.D., The Spiritual Prefect in Clerical Religious Houses of Study, X-140 pp., 1945.
217. Hynes, Rev. Harry Gerard, S.T.L., J.C.D., The Privileges of Cardinals, XII-183 pp., 1945.

218. McDevitt, Rev. Gerald Vincent, S.T.L., J.C.D., The Renunciation of an Ecclesiastical Office, XIV-179 pp., 1946.
219. Manning, Rev. Joseph Leroy, J.C.D., The Free Conferral of Offices, VII-116 pp., 1945.
220. Meyer, Rev. Louis G., O.S.B., A.B., S.T.B., J.C.D., Alms-Gathering by Religious, XII-163 pp., 1946.
221. O'Donnell, Rev. Cletus Francis, M.A., J.C.D., The Marriage of Minors, XII-268 pp., 1945.
222. Prunskis, Rev. Joseph, J.C.D., Comparative Law, Ecclesiastical and Civil in Lithuanian Concordat, X-161 pp., 1945.
223. Sweeney, Rev. Francis Patrick, C.Ss.R., J.C.D., The Reduction of Clerics to the Lay State, X-199 pp., 1945.
224. Vogelpohl, Rev. Henry John, J.C.D., The Simple Impediments to Holy Orders, XVI-190 pp., 1945.
225. Brockhaus, Rev. Thomas Aquinas, O.S.B., A.B., J.C.D., Religious who Are Known as Conversi, X-127 pp., 1945.
226. Griese, Rev. Nicholas Orville, S.T.D., J.C.D., Marriage and The Procreation of Offspring, XVI-224 pp., 1945.
227. Boudreaux, Rev. Warren Louis, J.C.D., The "ab acatholicis nati" of Canon 1099, § 2, XII-110 pp., 1946.
228. Bowe, Rev. Thomas Joseph, A.B., J.C.D., Religious Superioresses, VIII-206 pp., 1946.
229. Diederichs, Rev. Michael Ferdinand, S.C.J., J.C.D., The Jurisdiction of the Latin Ordinaries over their Oriental Subjects, XIV-153 pp., 1946.
230. Dingman, Rev. Maurice John, A.B., S.T.L., J.C.L., The Plaintiff in Contentious Trials.
231. Frison, Rev. Basil, C.M.F., M.Mus., J.C.D., The Retroactivity of Law, X-221 pp., 1946.
232. Galvin, Rev. William Anthony, M.A., J.C.D., The Administrative Transfer of Pastors, XII-288 pp., 1946.
233. Goracy, Rev. Joseph C., J.C.L., The Diriment Impediment of Major Orders.
234. Hale, Rev. Joseph Francis, M.A., S.T.L., J.C.L., The Pastor of Burial.
235. Henry, Rev. Joseph Arthur, A.B., J.C.D., The Mass and Holy Communion: Inter-Ritual Law, XII-138 pp., 1946.
236. Linenberger, Rev. Herbert, C.PP.S., J.C.L., The False Denunciation of an Innocent Confessor.
237. Lowry, Rev. James Martin, A.B., J.C.D., Dispensation from Private Vows, XII-266 pp., 1946.
238. Lynch, Rev. George Edward, A.B., S.T.L., J.C.D., Coadjutors and Auxiliaries of Bishops, X-107 pp., 1947.
239. Lynch, Rev. Timothy, M.S.SS.T., J.C.D., Contracts between Bishops and Religious Congregations, XIV-232 pp., 1946.

240. McClunn, Rev. Justin David, A.B., S.T.L., J.C.D., Administrative Recourse, VII-142 pp., 1946.
241. Lohmuller, Rev. Martin M., A.B., J.C.D., The Promulgation of Law, XII-140 pp., 1947.
242. McGrath, Rev. James, A.B., J.C.D., The Privilege of the Canon, XII-156 pp., 1946.
243. Marbach, Rev. Joseph Francis, A.B., J.C.D., Marriage Legislation for the Catholics of the Oriental Rites in the United States and Canada, XIV-314 pp., 1946.
244. Shimkus, Rev. Bernard Aloysius, A.B., J.C.L., The Determination and Transfer of Rite.
245. Smith, Rev. Vincent Michael, A.B., S.T.L., J.C.L., Ignorance Affecting Matrimonial Consent.
246. Wachtrle, Rev. Paul Anthony, A.B., J.C.L., The Baptism of the Children of Non-Catholics.
247. Crotty, Rev. Matthew M., J.C.D., The Recipient of First Holy Communion, X-142 pp., 1947.
248. Eagleton, Rev. George, J.C.L., The Quinquennial Faculties, Formula IV.
249. Gibbons, Rev. Marion L., C.M., LL.B., J.C.D., Domicile of The Wife Unlawfully Separated from Her Husband, XIV-171 pp., 1947.
250. Kelly, Rev. Bernard M., S.T.L., J.C.D., The Functions Reserved to Pastors, XII-141 pp., 1947.
251. Kilcullen, Rev. Thomas J., LL.M., J.C.D., The Collegiate Moral Person as Party Litigant, X-150 pp., 1947.
252. Lafonatine, Rev. Germain J., W.F., J.C.L., Relations Canoniques entre Le Missionnaire et Ses Superieurs.
253. Lane, Rev. Loras T., A.B., S.T.L., J.C.L., Matrimonial Procedure in the Ordinary Court of Second Instance.
254. Lover, Rev. James F., C.Ss.R., J.C.D., The Master of Novices, X-168 pp., 1947.
255. McNicholas, Rev. Timothy J., J.C.L., The Septimae Manus Witness.
256. Marositz, Rev. Joseph J., M.S.C., J.C.D., Obligations and Privileges of Religious Promoted to the Episcopal or Cardinalitial Dignities, XII-180 pp., 1947.
257. Murphy, Rev. Francis J., A.B., J.C.D., Legislative Powers of the Provincial Council, XII-158 pp., 1947.
258. O'Brien, Rev. Romaeus W., O.Carm., J.C.D., The Provincial Superior in Religious Orders of Men, X-294 pp., 1947.
259. Pfaller, Rev. Benedict A., O.S.B., J.C.L., The Ipso Facto Effected Dismissal of Religious.
260. Popek, Rev. Alphonse S., M.A., J.C.D., The Rights and Obligations of Metropolitans, XVIII-460 pp., 1947.
261. Ristuccia, Rev. Bernard J., C.M., J.C.L., Quasi-Religious Societies.

262. SONNTAG, REV. NATHANIEL L., O.F.M.CAP., J.C.D., Censorship of Special Classes of Books, XII-147 pp., 1947.
263. STADLER, REV. JOSEPH N., J.C.L., Frequent Holy Communion.
264. SZAL, REV. IGNATIUS J., J.C.L., The Communication of Catholics with Schismatics.
265. WAGNER, REV. URBAN S., O.F.M., CONV., J.C.D., Parochial Substitute Vicars and Supplying Priests, X-126 pp., 1947.
266. QUINN, REV. JOSEPH, M.A., J.C.L., Documents Required for the Reception of Orders.
267. BENNINGTON, REV. JAMES CLEMENT, A.B., J.C.L., The Recipient of Confirmation.
268. BLAHER, REV. DAMIAN JOSEPH, O.F.M., A.B., J.C.L., The Ordinary Processes in Causes of Beatification and Canonization.
269. CLUNE, REV. ROBERT BELL, A.B., J.C.L., The Judicial Interrogation of the Parties.
270. COURTMANCHE, REV. BASIL F., A.B., J.C.L., The Total Simulation of Matrimonial Consent.
271. DLOUHY, REV. MAUR JOHN, O.S.B., A.B., J.C.L., The Ordination of Exempt Religious.
272. DONOVAN, REV. JOHN THOMAS, PH.B., S.T.L., J.C.L., The Clerical Obligations of Canons 138 and 140.
273. FREKING REV. FREDERICK W., A.B., S.T.B., J.C.L., The Canonical Installation of Pastors.
274. FULTON, REV. THOMAS B., J.C.L., Prenuptial Investigation.
275. GODLEY, REV. JAMES P., J.C.L., The Time and the Place for the Celebration of Mass.
276. KANE, REV. THOMAS A., A.B., B.S., J.C.L., Jurisdiction of Patriarchs until 1439.
277. KENNEDY, REV. ANDREW A., J.C.L., The Annual Pastoral Report to the Local Ordinary.
278. KONRAD, REV. JOSEPH GEORGE, J.C.L., Transfer of Religious.
279. KRESS, REV. ALPHONSE, J.C.L., Contumacy in Ecclesiastical Trials.
280. MCCARTNEY, REV. MARCELLUS ANTHONY, O.F.M., M.A., J.C.L., Faculties of Regular Confessors.
281. MCCASLIN, REV. EDWARD PATRICK, M.A., S.T.L., J.C.L., The Division of Parishes.
282. MCELROY, REV. FRANCIS J., A.B., J.C.L., The Privileges of Bishops.
283. QUINN, REV. STEPHEN, M.S.SS.T., J.C.L., Relation between the Local Ordinary and Religious of Diocesan Approval.
283. SCHNEIDER, REV. EDELHARD LOUIS, S.D.S., A.B., J.C.L., The Status of Secularized ex-Religious Clerics.
284. THOMPSON, REV. CHESTER J., A.B., J.C.L., The Simple Removal from Office.

www.ingramcontent.com/pod-product-compliance
Lightning Source LLC
LaVergne TN
LVHW050203080826
844660LV00012B/340

* 9 7 8 0 8 1 3 2 2 4 5 4 1 *